Log Hut

By the Same Author

I BOUGHT A MOUNTAIN

I BOUGHT A STAR

A COUNTRY OF MEMORABLE HONOUR

Log Hut

THOMAS FIRBANK

GEORGE G. Harrap & CO. LTD
LONDON TORONTO WELLINGTON SYDNEY

60713

First published in Great Britain 1954
by GEORGE G. HARRAP & CO. LTD
182 High Holborn, London, W.C.1

*Composed in Fournier type and printed by Western Printing Services Ltd.,
Bristol
Made in Great Britain*

PREFACE

I HAVE been from Shallows for quite a long time, and have since lived with Chinese, Malays, Indians, Dyaks, Indonesians, and remnants of races difficult to name. These many Eastern peoples differ profoundly from each other in blood, language, creed, and customs. In addition they differ from the West in the wide range of human values, except one: the value of home.

The attap huts, stilted river dwellings, communal long houses, and wooden town hovels of the East are pooled with the desirable Western residences as the common property of mankind.

To-day my host is squatting below his hut platform by the charcoal embers, shaking the frying rice spread on the lid of a biscuit tin. Presently he will offer me my share, and his too if I want it. He is a proud man, as jealous of the good name of his house as ever I have been of mine.

A family's home is its wall against the world, the fortress for its children, and the armour which protects its ego. The building absorbs an essence from the occupiers which, when they are absent, craves for a rejoining to make completeness once more.

I am half-way round the earth from Shallows, but something of me is drawn to something of me which is left there. Yet, like the crab, humans have this versatility, that when we have left the one shell we grow another. Presently the new one fits, and we call it home.

THOMAS FIRBANK

CHIANG MAI
NORTH THAILAND
March 1954

CONTENTS

CHAPTER THIRTEEN

Holly—The scavenger—Midland market—A feast for the birds—Gift boxes—Covent Garden success—Poltergeist—Chanterelles and other fungi

CHAPTER FOURTEEN

The peat set—Bill Waters—Difficulties: rough tracks, weather, and lack of capital—The tramway—The granulator—Unfriendly moor—The end of three years' work

CHAPTER FIFTEEN

Cord-moss—Ferns—Maize—The onion flower—Meadow sage—Peas and brooms—Monkey musk and sunflower—Arum lilies—Life at Shallows

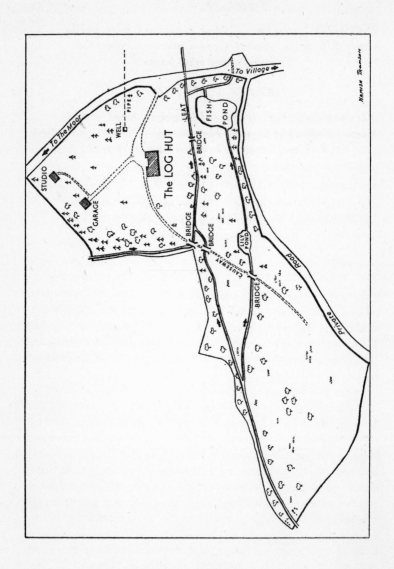

HAMISH TRENTERN

To Village →

To The Moor →

WELL
PIPE

STUDIO

GARAGE

The LOG HUT

LEAT

BRIDGE

BRIDGE

FISH POND

BRIDGE

BRIDGE

LILY POND

CAUSEWAY

BRIDGE

Private Road

CHAPTER ONE

*An advertisement—The man with the bill-hook—Shallows: the
house, the garden, the wood—Indecision—We make up our minds*

I SAW the advertisement in the local paper. It said:

FOR SALE with immediate possession. Colonial style bunga-
low of unusual character. Timber and stone construction.
Comprising 4 bed., 2 rec., usual offices. Own elec. Magnificent
natural gardens extending to five acres with woodland, meadow,
orchard, two streams, waterfalls, fish- and lily-ponds, garage,
studio, linhays. Situated in sought-after Rattleford area.
1000 ft. above sea-level.

I passed the paper over the hotel breakfast-table to Tessa, who
pushed my thumb aside and read without comment. I said defen-
sively that the place sounded fun. She answered that so had
Westhay, North Nymph, Hollowcombe, Nathill, Blackworthy, and
Yardbeer, also two score others whose names she had deliberately
forgotten.

In the end we went in the jeep.

Rattleford lay close under the north-east edge of Dartmoor, and
a corner of the moor lay between us. The map showed clearly that
a long main-road circumnavigation might be avoided by mounting
over the barrier along a series of lanes. A woman believes in a map
about as much as a Nonconformist in the infallibility of the Pope,
and Tessa became mistrustful of the gated and unsignposted tracks
which ran across the heathland, or drove like mole runs through
tunnels arched with rowan and hazel. It was a stormy day indeed
for midsummer, and presently she suggested that, as we did not seem
to be arriving at any particular place, we should make off in a direction which would lay the wind on another quarter. It was,
apparently, on her side that the rain blew in. The children, on the

hard back seat, added complaints about cold, damp, jolting, and incipient hunger. I would have turned back had the map shown me how.

It was then that we came for the first time upon the topographical illusion of Gidleigh. Many a signpost we had seen that morning which stabbed a finger towards Gidleigh, and several times we must have been within hooting distance of the hamlet, just as a bedevilled sightseer passes and repasses within feet of the centre of a maze.

Several lanes met secretively at a spot marked by a church and a couple of bungalows which formed the heart of Gidleigh. Two of the roads were marked to Rattleford. I took the broader and gave promise to my passengers of drinks and ice-cream. I felt like a modern Columbus, saved from mutiny by the timely sight of land-birds and the floating flotsam of shallow waters. I drove speedily for a few minutes, and entered a village. Though the church had now moved to the other hand, we all recognized Gidleigh again. There remained, however, the lesser lane. By this route our return to the church took longer, but was no less inevitable.

I was reading the map when a man with a bill-hook came through the hedge. Time and space had lost consequence for me, and I was prepared to accept the stranger as a fugitive from Sedgemoor and the justice of Bloody Jeffreys.

Tessa at once inquired the road to Rattleford.

"Be you'm wanting short road or long road?" asked the man.

We said, simultaneously, that any road would do.

The man waved his implement at the lesser lane. The way the blade curved round to point at the church was an ominous symbolism of our circular journeying.

"'Tis that 'un'll take 'ee quickest."

I said that I had tried it and that it would not take us at all.

"Ah!" he said. "You'm'll've followed 'un round, 'stead of keeping on up t'hill."

I replied that the divergence to the hill was marked "Impracticable for Motors." The man laughed heartily.

"'Tis a praaper good road over t'hill," he said. "Don't 'ee take no notice of t'old board. You try 'ee."

We tried 'ee, and broke our bondage. In no time at all we came

to Rattleford, and the trip begun under evil auspices was coloured
by bright omens. We came out from under the rain-clouds, which
had by now vented their spite on the seaward side of the moor.
The sun shone clear, and the village was gay.

There was an old market-house in the square, a hexagonal building, whose facets housed a greengrocer, a one-legged cobbler, a
taxi office, an antique-dealer, and the public lavatories. I thought
that this versatility argued a breadth of outlook in the parish
council.

There was a large number of cars about, but more riding-horses.
There were farmers flapping on bare-backed cobs; well-breeched
folk of high status on hunters; children on lazy, tubby ponies.
Horses were hitched to railings, and to car bumpers. Horses' heads,
at the end of a rein, followed their dismounted riders into the shops.
The men busy about their morning errands were dressed so shab-
bily that they were obviously of superior breeding and education.
The dogs at heel were predominantly labradors and spaniels. The
older women wore drab felt hats; but the younger coloured
trousers.

Tessa and I, more cheerful in the expansive climate of this
sheltered side of Dartmoor, went into an inn to ask directions to our
house advertised as 'Shallows.'

"'Tisn't no place I never heard of," said one of the company.
"Likely 'tis Gidleigh way."

I assured him that we were well acquainted with Gidleigh, and
had viewed the church and houses from most directions. One
fellow ruminated for the space of a tankard, and said suddenly:

"'Tis Log 'Ut you want!"

"Little Kinglet, 'tis now," another asserted.

"Maybe. But 'twas Log 'Ut time agone, and 'tisn't Little Kinglet
no more. Young Army chap bought it. Likely 'tis Shallows now."

"Aye. Terrible place for water."

"Terrible place it is for bushes, tuw."

I got my directions, sure that I would recognize the place when
I came upon a stilted lake-dwelling in a jungle.

The lane to which we had been commended rose steadily towards
the skyline of the moor, whose eminence set it above the tree-tops

of the valley. The skyline directly ahead was pointed by the massive beheaded pyramid of Kestor Rock. Within the two miles between Rock and vale lay a cross-section of English countryside. There was the village of Rattleford, sprawled in the crook of a sheltering ridge; there was the river Teign, slow-flowing, tree-lined, strung with easy meadows; then, as we climbed, there came woods of conifers and hardwoods mixed, and between them open swards studded with granite boulders, and dotted with tall bracken clumps. We came close below the rim of the moor and crossed the Teign once more. Here was a river of very different character from the idling stream of the lowland. Here the river had gained strength after its birth not so far above, but had not yet learned continence. It frothed and leapt and fretted with the impetuosity of all youth. It boiled down through the trees on our left hand, dived beneath the road, and plunged headlong into the deep-carved gorge to the right.

Within a few furlongs we had come from the sedateness of the valley to the wildness of the upland. The north-east apron of the moor flattened momentarily, and here we found Shallows, one of several dwellings strung along the mile of level shelf. We left the jeep outside the gate and walked the short distance up the driveway. From the first we did not look on the property as a house and its garden, but as a garden in which a house happened to have grown. A more haphazard house we had never seen, and its very inconsequence and lack of rectilinear shape fitted it the less conspicuously into the natural surround.

The garden distracted the eye from the building by showing infinite variety. We had time to notice a tall bamboo clump, fronded and graceful, which swayed and rustled at the call of the wind eddies which spilled off the moor. There were tall azaleas and dwarf ones; some single, some in clumps of a score or two. There were tight communities of lissom golden cypress, which danced to every quirk of air. There were miniature forests of the osmunda, the royal fern, with its khaki flowers. Two rhododendron shrubberies were thirty feet in height, domed like great multi-greened beehives. Beyond them towered a dark green Wellingtonia. Beside the house was a delicate thuya. It was no ordinary thuya, for the roots had surfaced, and from them several stems had sported upward, so that a cluster of smaller trees thronged about the central trunk like chicks around a hen. The tips of the group merged into a perfect point, and from a short distance the copse looked like one lone tree.

There was no time to take in more, but I had already experienced that inevitability of intimate friendship which comes sometimes in new human relationships before ever one has time even to say more than a word or two. I was a part of this place.

The frontage at which we arrived was confusing. There was first the gable end of a substantial wooden wing; then a porch draped with honeysuckle set beside an ancient rounded chimney in the shape of a pottery kiln; then a long low stretch, windowed like a railway-carriage, running on a different line to both gable and porch; then another porch; then, on a different line, a granite gable end; and, beyond, a wooden protuberance with double doors which was not a garage, since it was one step above ground.

I went to the nearer porch and knocked. Presently I heard the door of the farther porch open. We moved along, heard the door shut as we went, and as we arrived the first door opened. This went on for some time, as some agency within the house moved to and fro out of time with our own shuttling. It was an experience to which we were to become well accustomed later, with ourselves playing the part within the house. At last, tiring, I opened the door in the first porch, and found myself looking across a square hall-way into a bathroom where a lady was washing herself at the basin. This sort of situation too was one with which we were, from the house point of view, to become familiar.

It was now that the unseen person who was opening and shutting the outer doors coincided with us. He was the owner, and the lady his wife. We were led up a step through the room with the railway-carriage window effect, up another step into a hall whose cross-section was that of a ridge tent, and up one more step into a sitting-room which was the granite wing. The steps were no more than the expression of an architect who skipped for *joie de vivre*, since the whole conglomeration was strung together on perfectly level ground. The room with the carriage windows was, we noticed in passing, surprisingly attractive inside, being L-shaped, with the inner leg of the L evidently playing the devil with the layout of the rooms parallel with it. It was furnished as a dining-room, and had a sloping roof on three levels, lined with tongue-and-groove boarding. The walls were panelled in really good oak. It appeared, however, to be more a passage than a room, for it was the only link between the two halls, and I imagined my meals growing cold as I rushed from outer door to door to catch an inconvenient visitor.

The sitting-room was an eye-opener. It filled the entire stone end of the house, with windows cunningly in all four walls, and had a high roof like a tithe-barn. We were impressed at once, and at great pains not to show it.

It is a difficult experience to look over a house with the possibility that one may purchase it, for the technique required of the viewer is different from the inspection of a friend's dwelling. The friend remarks casually that you have never seen over the place, have you? You say that no, but you have always enviously wished to do so. The host leads the way from room to room, with laughing arguments about precedence in the doorways. His remarks are deprecating, as might be those of a well-bred Chinese in similar circumstances. Yours are ecstatic. You begin to sympathize with the problems of inspecting royalty, as you grope for the apt remark. Your host too is feeling the strain by the time he comes to denigrate the boot-hole. In the end both of you march back to the den and drink spirits with the sudden wordless companionship of men who have shared an ordeal.

But when purchase is in the air your hyperbole becomes tinged with spite, and the owner's deprecation with conceit. You are shown a beautiful spare bedroom scented with fresh flowers, polished, speckless, new magazines and a biscuit barrel on the table. It is a pity no one has been in for a few days, says your guide. It is quite a nice room when it is clean and aired.

You say that you wish your spare room was as beautifully kept. The only advantage yours has is that it is next door to the bathroom and has rather a nice built-in wardrobe.

This diplomatic level of thrust and parry cannot long be maintained. You come to a study with egress to hall, sitting-room, and garden. You are told, with a laugh, how convenient it is to have a bolt-hole with so many entrances. You agree, and add that you dare say it is not too cold in winter if you screw up two of the doors and nail felt over them.

The pair of you end the tour by snarling compliments like brickbats concealed in bouquets.

Tessa and I sat in the sitting-room with the young owner and his wife. The two children also sat, but with the ominous quiet of a couple of ticking bombs. Tessa's nerve broke, and she asked permission to turn them loose in the garden. We heard a diminishing volume of sound as they went, then silence.

Our host led me to the larger set of windows, filling all the south wall of the sitting-room, under pretext of showing the view; but in reality, I suspect, that I might notice the ripening figs on the tree whose topmost leaves lay on the sill as if it were a wardrobe shelf in Eden. Immediately beyond a sloping lawn was a small stream spanned by a simple plank bridge, and beyond again was a large weedy pool which was, I guessed, the fish-pond. I saw both our children, thoughtfully shoeless, dabbling in the stream in a squatting fashion, so that the seats of their pants and the rear hems of their dresses were in the water. Tessa, I was glad to see, was talking to the bathroom lady about tradesmen, and did not notice.

We went through the house. There was, I now found, no need to use the dining-room as a passage during meals, since the three bedrooms between the two halls led from one to the other, though, by an architectural sleight of doors, they could be entered severally or separately from one or other hall and from the veranda. I did not then know it, but I was to be confused by this domestic geography for at least a year, and only became oriented after I had boarded up some of the apertures.

The centre bedroom of those three which adjoined like the scenery of a French farce was delightful. Like the sitting-room, it had a pitched ceiling with big skylight; a window on to the wistaria-shaded veranda; a glazed door to give egress to the wistaria; and a very good stone fireplace. I saw it at once as a study, and still do, but have failed to dispossess the children.

There was but one lavatory, though it was separate from, and,

B

indeed, more spacious than, the bathroom. This was a favourable point, since in houses where bathing and eliminatory facilities are combined our children suffer a gastric loosening immediately one reclines in the bath, and hammer for admittance under penalty of mishap else.

The kitchen and main bedroom filled what an agent would describe as the west wing; that was the wooden counterpart at the opposite end to the granite sitting-room. Both kitchen and bedrooms were large and well lighted. This seemed the time to ask about water. There was an electric pump which drew from a well and filled the roof cistern, and the water, as we were given documentary proof, stood high in the esteem of the public analyst. A neat stove, colloquially called a cook-and-heat, performed the two functions of warming the hot-water cylinder and cooking the food.

We went outside. Tessa was thinking a few years ahead about a pony for the children, and asked where the meadow lay. She was told she was on it, likewise she was in the orchard. The meadow, we then realized, was a patch of rough grass a little larger than a double tennis-court. Two old, unpruned apple-trees grew out of it, and several little upstart plum- and pear-trees, which were obviously newcomers. We crossed the meadow, passed between the two giant clumps of rhododendrons, walked under the enormous Wellingtonia, whose bark clung in great flakes like slabs of cork, and came to the studio. It really was a studio, with an enormous window on the one side only, to gather the pure north light. There was a closed stove, and I thought how excellent a lair the building would make for children, as it was within but distant earshot of the house.

The garage was near by, and the electric-light plant lay in it with an air of inanimate malevolence. The dynamo generated at fifty volts, feeding by overhead wires a set of batteries which were installed in a lean-to against the side wall of the sitting-room. The set was fairly modern, and I saw no difficulty in its operation.

I asked to see the linhays, but since I pronounced the name just as written, my guide was much puzzled. After a lengthy misunderstanding I discovered that the word was said as 'linny.' The linhays were galvanized-iron structures like miniature Dutch barns. One was beside the garage drive, and promised supplementary car storage; one was beside the garage, inaccessible in a jungle of giant laurels which rose out of an age-old accumulation of rotting tree-trimmings, whose felled trunks, cross-cut into pieces only four or five feet long, lay heaped like huge cotton-reels; the third linhay was quite near the house, and contained coal in one half and a built-in dog-kennel in the other.

Our hosts asked if we would like to see the rest of the ground, and seemed a little disturbed when we said we would. One of the reasons for their hesitation was apparent when Tessa became immobilized in a bog close by the coal linhay. Some time was lost while both sides apologized confusedly that there had been heavy rain lately; that it was very stupid of Tessa to step just there; that after rain the water soon drained off, but they ought to have thought; that Tessa could take off her shoes in the jeep and put her feet in an old sack.

We pressed on, laughing in rather a strained way. We followed the bank of the stream which owned the plank bridge, coming soon to a grassy patch from which grew an old oak which, though of moderate height, showed a tremendous spread of branches. The limbs twisted and contorted against the sky as if an imprisoned nymph were supplicating relief from the bole. High up in a fork was wedged a tea-chest in which an owl had made a home until the box was tilted by a gale.

At this side of the house was none of the stately stillness of the studio part, which had been dignified by the presence of massive conifers, whose stature and poise had been copied by the flowering shrubs. Here all was coloured by the sparkle and movement of water. The two streams, fresh-run from the moor above, burst out of the patch of woodland. They turned and doubled and leapt with the inconsequence of flirting hares. They spouted over waterfalls, slid slowly through big pools, frothed over shallow gravel, and with a final flourish vanished under the lane beyond the fish-pond on their way to the Teign deep in its gorge.

There was sparkle and liveliness everywhere as we walked between the streams towards the wood. We passed a buddleia, the butterfly tree, a-quiver with shimmering wings of many colours. Here and there the osmunda grew in head-high clumps on the water's edge, the fronds of the royal fern artificial in the precision of their outline. Astilbes revelled in the moisture which bathed their roots. The long lily-pond was spanned by big stepping-stones, and when we stood on them to look down into the water the idle trout hardly took notice of us, and drifted but slowly under the screen of the lily-leaves.

We were now at the fringe of the wood, but ingress was barred to the ladies by a fence of wire netting intertwined with, and reinforced for ten feet behind by, a rolling, coiled barrier of head-high brambles, through which tall nettles strove to reach the light.

Our host said that there was the wood, beyond the fence. I asked to go around its boundary, and thereby evoked a fleeting glance of apprehension, followed by a set look of determination. We left the women, and went along the entanglement to the boundary hedge. On its far side a bridle-path led up to the moor. Next the hedge a gate, hung from a rude pillar of lichened stone, opened directly into the brambles. We trod our way through, giving voice to many a hearty quip, and making many assurances to one another that all was well; that these were old trousers; that it was only a scratch.

It was apparent that to enter deep into the wood was impracticable, and we kept up an open ride beside the bridle-path, whose only obstacles were bracken and fallen timber. The bridle-path was insecurely fenced from us by a few sagging strands of barbed wire, strung between oaks and tall hollies, but the track was sunk in a deep gully, water-worn down the middle, and my host assured me that it was gated where it joined the motor-lane by the house, and again where it debouched on the moor; so that no animals frequented it.

The top boundary of the wood was fenced with a fine rabbit-proof erection by the Forestry Commission, who had just planted a small area between us and the moor, whose even skyline showed above us through the last rank of trees. At the point where we reached the Forestry corner the Shallows wood was of very young growth. There was a patch of about a third of an acre in which grew no large trees, but only saplings, bracken, and brambles, and I thought at once that it might be possible to reclaim this area either to kitchen garden or pasture. My host looked at me as if I were queer, but agreed that you could, he supposed, reclaim anything if you put your mind to it.

It proved impossible to follow the Forestry fence, and to return down the other boundary. It was to be three years before I did so. We returned to the house by the way we had come.

Tessa, who was at that time prone to colds, was in the kitchen, sniffing, and the children were unwillingly by the cook-and-heat steaming. We collected ourselves, and went out towards the jeep. I had no idea what Tessa thought of the place, though Louise kept poking at me with her finger and demanding when we were to move in. Johanna too, though still at an inarticulate age, made her wishes clear.

I dropped behind the damp procession and asked my host how much he really wanted for the place, and explained that though it was, of course, quite delightful, after all most of the house was only of clapboard; one had to pump the water; private lighting plants were always temperamental; the wood was really of no practical use or value; one of the linhays was buried in jungle; the immediate purlieus of the house were boggy; the fish-pond was full of weeds; the streams probably flooded; the lily-pool wanted clearing out; at least one tree was liable to fall on the house; the orchard would not produce for years; the meadow could not maintain more than a couple of rabbits in a creeper; there were so many intercommunicating doors within the house that it must be both noisy and draughty; and the bathroom was very small. Otherwise I thought we rather liked what we had seen.

I was prepared to do a bit of horse-dealing about price, and to go away with non-committal assurances to write further. But the young man made no protest against my strictures, nor comment on my desire to bargain. He said simply that it was a happy place, and must always have been thus to have so marked a carefree atmosphere; and that if I had not fallen in love with it some one would and that when that happened they would buy without quibble.

We drove in silence for some distance on the homeward way. This time it was not the sad silence which usually followed upon house inspection, but a reflective quietude. At length I remarked tentatively that there had certainly been something attractive about the place, though the house was inconvenient, and the garden semi-derelict. Tessa came out of a reverie to say that the house was inconvenient, and the garden semi-derelict, but that there was something attractive about the place. Whereupon verbally we tore the house and its amenities to shreds, laughing that any fond owner dared so much as to advertise for sale, let alone fix a price at double the worth. We fought against a favourable emotion as a gay bachelor struggles against a serious inamorata, or a nervous wayfarer whistles by night to keep away the intangibles which may lay hold upon his spirit.

When at last we arrived back at our inn on the bleak western side of the moor—a side so different in character to that on which Shallows lay—we had exhausted our fund of vituperation, just as two abusive people can at last find no more to say about a third party. Here Louise chipped in to remark that the house with the streams was the nicest of all, and that, speaking for herself, and for Johanna who could not, there existed no other worth-while house in the world.

Tessa and I went to bed more than half decided to buy, and we had even discussed, in that panic-stricken way of people hovering about an open sale, whether to ring up lest some one else came along to fall in love with the inconveniences. But morning brought sterner counsel. Away from the appeal, we remembered only the faults. And yet I was snared, for never before had a place touched me so intimately. It was not as a house alone that I thought of the property, for house and garden could not be disentangled. They were an entity. I did not feel that some one could tend the ground by draining, by rooting out brambles and nettles, by clearing fallen timber, by practising kind surgery on injured trees, by letting air and light into choked shrubberies. This was not work for some one, but for me.

Tessa and I went again to look. Our eyes remained wide open to the faults, but the place had a powerful, active spirit which laid hold on us still more firmly. Even now we did not buy, resenting, perhaps, this very hold gained by the inanimate.

It was from London, three months later, that I was impelled to telephone a firm offer. I learned that I had no longer first refusal, and must await while another man decided yes or no. All of us then knew an agony of desire for what had become less certainly obtainable and we spent a week in heart-ache and recriminations. Tessa and I blamed each the other, the children both of us. We were a miserable family until the vendor rang to say that the sale was again open. I haggled half-heartedly, saved my face with the concession of a few pounds, and bought.

We moved in during November, a few weeks later.

CHAPTER TWO

A sheltered position—Log Hut and Little Kinglet—Problem of surface water—Bert Westmacott—Westhill Water Supply—Robertson of Westhill—Electric-light plants—Land-drains and water-courses—First spring

THE first thing we noticed was that winter did not lay bleak fingers on our garden. To begin with, we gave thanks to the climate of the West Country, which a preconceived idea told us was mild. Soon we discounted this theory, for above us, below us, and not far away on either side of us, the stripped bones of trees shivered in the wind which poured like an unseen ice-fall over the edge of the moor. And our bones, too, felt the chill when we went a few hundred yards outside our garden. We learned that the high ground of the West Country was a winter tilting-ground for the Atlantic gales, whose earliest landfall it was

After a while we found that we owed thanks not to the climate for immunity from winter storms, but to a freak of the contours which had isolated us from wind, but left us open from dawn to dusk to any and every gleam of sunshine. Many times we knew that a gale was plaguing our neighbours. We knew because the topmost tips of our tallest trees were arched like bows. These aerial outposts whistled the news of storm to the untroubled vegetation below.

The vegetation itself helped the illusion that for us there was no winter. When the deciduous trees and shrubs shed their leaves they seemed to shrink for cover among the predominant evergreens. They were concealed by the firs, pines, thuyas, and spruces; by the many kinds of tall, red-berried hollies; by the varied greens of the rhododendrons; by the orange-fruited berberis; and by the lily-of-the-valley trees, the flame-tipped andromedas.

A few days after our arrival I was leaning over the drive gate.

I was noting how even the bareness of the oaks was softened by ample cloaks of bottle-green ivy and veils of lichen shaded in pastel colours beyond the ingenuity of the dyer. The bole of the nearest oak was circled with flowering cyclamen which mounted with the moss up to the bark itself. The buds of azaleas and rhododendrons denied that this was November. I was not then much of a shrub-gardener, and did not realize how closely these new buds had followed the drop of the last flower petal.

The morning postman disturbed me.

"'Tis a praaper fine day," he said, and lingered a moment, leaning on his ash-stave.

"Be you'm for altering name again?" he asked. "Little Kinglet 'twas before they last people a-christened it Shallows."

I said that I saw no reason to change.

"'Twon't make ha'poorth difference, anyway," said postman. "Log 'Ut 'twill always be."

Yet we had already discovered that the building was not a dwelling-place at all. It was neither hut, cottage, nor mansion. It had just happened in the garden, as an arbour might. We went within to sleep, and to perform some of the duties laid upon us by progress; to write letters, telephone, or change our clothes. But we looked on the building as no more than a part of the garden. We passed through it as a short cut from one place to another, for there were so many doors in both long sides that it never got in our way.

However, the house was not negligible. It had a personality of active happiness which was not distinguishable from that of the garden, for house and garden had grown up together. The land had been part of a small estate a half-century before. The squire had perhaps noticed how that small pocket of ground obeyed none of the harsher laws of climate, but dreamed the year through in tranquillity. He built a gardener's hut and began to plant shrubs and ferns and specimen conifers of many kinds. As the trees grew to handsome youth another member of the squire's family added a little to the hut and lived in it from time to time.

Then the estate was broken up. By now the sheltered and more mature garden was the home of many birds, and the property was bought by a man who studied them, who added again to the house, and who renamed it Little Kinglet, after the goldcrested wren. He endowed it with the love of living creatures, just as it had already been endowed with the love of growing plants. So the place was when we came; loved and loving.

The aura of humans settles thickest about the spots in which they live. Their hopes and dreads; their happiness and misery; their passions, good and evil, permeate the bricks and stones, and linger in the air above much walked paths. There are homesteads which have little to say; and some which tell wickedness; and some which speak goodness. Whether you called our new home Log 'Ut, Little Kinglet, or Shallows, it replied always with kindness.

The kindness, however, was sometimes rough and ready. Shallows kept us up to the mark by manifesting faults and irritating habits which saved it from cloying perfection. We had not been unaware of these when we bought. The knowledgeable ale-drinkers of the local inns had told us that the house floated on water, like a raft. Also a surveyor had looked over the place for us. He had put a few words on a half-sheet of paper, but, being a West Country-man, had tired, and made his main report by word of mouth. The gist of it was that the roof would bear watching.

We did not then know of the casual, *laissez-faire* characteristics of Devon folk. We thought that no more was said because there was no more to say. We were delighted that faults were so few, and contrasted the report with one rendered to us by a London surveyor years before when we were negotiating for a house in Chelsea. We had almost broken off the preliminaries when this folio was presented to us. It was an inch or two thick, and it seemed obvious that nothing could be right. We thumbed over a few pages and found that the subject-matter dealt with lost door-keys, cracked window-panes, frayed electric flex, and even the faded patches on the wall-paper. The cost of the two surveys was identical, but had our London man done the Shallows survey, he would have been writing yet. However, lost keys would not have mattered at Shallows, because we never lock our doors; nor frayed cables, because we cannot shock ourselves off our anæmic fifty volts.

In fact, we would have bought Shallows even if the committee of the Surveyors' Institute had banded together to send us a black-edged warning. When two people fall in love the family of neither, in all its wisdom and experience, can put the one off the other. It is sometimes the same between house and would-be buyer.

The rains came during our first month, and not even the garden of Shallows was exempt. Indeed, it attracted more surface-water than its share, for an old map, plotting what it called the 'water-easements,' showed that every stream in the neighbourhood converged upon our wood and joined one of our two streams. Here and there springs were flooded into life and spurted up through the undergrowth like geysers; and patches of turf, formerly firm, quaked underfoot. Worse still, the dining-room flooded. A few of the surveyor's roof-leaks dripped on to its floor, but most of the water welled up from below in an underhand manner which it was impossible to combat by direct action like plugging a hole in the roof.

We had lived in gum-boots for some days when I met Bert Westmacott as I was trying to do something about a water-course which was surging down the drive and out under the gate.

Bert lived in a cottage down the lane. He was a tall, well-built man, dark as a gypsy, with fine bones and features which showed that there was good blood in him. We both knew who the other was by country grape-vine, and wasted no time on introductions.

"'Tis they trees," said Bert, hitching his wet sack round his shoulders. "If 'twas me I'd tear 'em down. 'Tis naught they do but draw the rain."

I refused to contemplate the destruction of the trees, and said that lack of proper ditches was the trouble.

"Ditches won't do no harm," Bert agreed. "Come Monday I'll give 'ee a hand." He turned up on Monday, stayed two years on full time, and materializes still whenever summat's to be done.

Bert was a man of big ideas. He showed at once that he wished to excavate great embanked ditches, linked one with the other in a complicated system like the German canals. I was more subtle, having been schooled in the hills of Wales. It seemed to me that nearly every morass resulted from some recurrent spring which came to life in sympathy with rain, and that if we found and tapped the springs the ground about them would become firm.

I started Bert in the quagmire where Tessa had foundered on our very first visit. He began the day in Wellingtons, but appeared after lunch in thigh-boots, which were not so readily sucked off. We dug experimentally here and there. Our trenches filled with water, but only with a steady oozing, not the spurt of the oil-gusher which I sought, until late in the day I came on a rock, as I thought, and took a pick to it. The object broke readily, and to my superstitious astonishment began to spray me, immovable as I was in the mud, with a jet of water. Bert feared none of the elementals of the moor, and wallowed in beside me to give the thing beneath the slime a good wallop. That really annoyed it, and it spurted in all directions.

"'Tis a rare case?" exclaimed Bert, and felt down with his hands. He surfaced with a piece of terra-cotta piping.

"A drain 'tis! Now whatever for be there a drain down in here?"

Drenched with water beyond further care, we tracked the pipe backward to a brick cistern. Under the turf was a steel man-hole, which we lifted and cleaned. Embossed on its lid were the words: "Westhill Water Supply."

"Now we've done it!" I said to Bert.

Westhill was the big house across the lane, where once had lived the proprietor of the estate who had put up the original cabin of Log 'Ut.

Bert's face showed more concern at this threat of the physical rather than at the earlier supernatural manifestation, but he rallied after a moment.

"Us'll bury 'un all up quick," he decided. "Westhill's empty anyway." We agreed on this without too great a sense of guilt, because we had seen that the pipe was leaking at every joint. We did not think that our excavations had done all that much to make matters worse.

However, before we buried 'un all up quick, we cut a deep ditch from the cistern to the nearest stream, laid a double row of four-inch land-drains, and put the earth back on top of them. Bert was distressed at filling-in. He maintained that you could not tell that a fellow had been digging.

The affair lay uneasily on my conscience. I felt like a remorseful murderer who has planted the remains of his victim under the cabbages. But the extraordinary thing was that good came out of evil, for the flood in the dining-room receded and finally dried up. We had obviously cut off at the source the subterranean water-supply, and Tessa was delighted until I blurted out the story of the cistern. After a day or two she suggested that we should stroll over to have a look at Westhill. She pretended that she felt merely normal feminine curiosity about an empty house, but I knew quite well that she was prompted by guilt now that she had become an accessory. She felt a morbid urge to wander about the place so greatly affected by the crime.

However, on the way up Westhill drive Tessa's mind was distracted. She noted a shrub or two which Shallows lacked, and I took a few cuttings with my penknife. We told one another that the bushes were badly in need of pruning, and that we were doing Westhill a good service. Fringing a pond near the front door was a saxifrage with broad leaves like a water-plantain, a Megasea, which we saw was a winter-flowering variety. The pink petals grew in tight clusters between the leaves. It was not quite the season, but we could see that the clumps were overcrowded, and that we ought to thin them. We did so, slicing through the thick, fleshy stems, which were covered with flaky brown skin, like bad cigars.

Thus laden, we crossed the gravel sweep towards the front windows of Westhill. I stepped on a flower-bed, pressed my nose against a window, and peered within. About an inch away a pair of fierce eyes stared back into mine. I recoiled upon Tessa. The window opened and a head appeared, whose mouth inquired without preliminary whether I knew anything about engines. I said, a little wildly, that I did; that we did not know Westhill was now occupied; that we were taking a stroll.

"Wait!" ordered the owner of the head. Freezing us, he vanished. He came out of the front door, and approached with an old-world charm of manner, to which Tessa replied with a kind of bow, hands filled with greenery behind her back, like a nervous child prodded to present a bouquet. I saw that the ferocity had gone out of the stranger's eyes, introduced ourselves, and learned that our new neighbour was named Robertson. In the course of a talk, politely inquisitive on both sides, we found out that the old chap was seventy years of age—although he only showed sixty of them—and that he had been Scottish Prime Minister of an Indian native state. He had ranked seventy-eight servants, including one who preceded him on formal occasions bearing a golden orb on a cushion. Robertson, therefore, had not found it necessary to learn much about the meaner characteristics of engines.

We found the thing lurking in a shed. It was nearly coeval with its new owner, and presented many features of design with which I, born in a later generation, was unfamiliar. Robertson obviously regarded me as a white hope, and watched with childlike confidence as I fiddled gingerly with taps and switches. He explained that they had had practically no light the previous evening because the batteries were nearly exhausted; and, worse still, no water. This last news reminded us of the pick-axed pipe, and confirmed our worst fears. We discovered, however, that the ostensible reason for the lack of water was that the electric pump would not operate until the engine went.

With the Prime Minister's eye upon me, I tried every possible permutation of the controls, and for a half-hour swung at the handle until my palm was raw. I felt that I owed it to him. As failure succeeded failure, I imagined the old man pining for his seventy-eight servants, who would have filled his cistern with a chain of buckets quicker than the engine and I. I could also feel Tessa praying for me; hoping that by performance of this service we could claim some offset for the destruction of the water-supply.

I had just about given up all hope of success when a negligent and exhausted swing at the handle touched some finer feeling in the cantankerous machine. With a wheeze and a groan it began to chuff. Robertson was delighted. I could imagine him repeating to some old crony: "These young fellows are every bit as good as we were in our day, Arbuthnot." Then I remembered about the water. It was more likely that Robertson would say: "The country's changed since we were at school, Arbuthnot. No respect for property now. These young hooligans smash your place up as soon as you take your eye off them."

Robertson asked us to wait just a moment to see if the water-pump worked, while Tessa and I stood like felons on the drop until he reappeared, all smiles. The pump was delivering at gallons a minute, and we must return for a drink in a day or two when the house was straighter.

Tessa retrieved our plants and cuttings from behind a bush, and went off home much puzzled by the complexities of the Westhill water-tables.

Electric-light plants were as valid a conversational subject around our parts as were servants in suburbia. On a visit to anyone's house we learned to inquire how the set was doing, and to listen patiently to complaints or eulogies. If the lights were on we would sit and watch the flicker of the bulbs, and diagnose symptoms. The Shallows set was, perhaps, over-simple. Certainly it had no refinements, and the engine had to be started by hand. An affinity grew between it and me, and it always behaved perfectly, but it would do nothing for Bert Westmacott or anyone else. It kicked them with the handle, ran backward, squirted oil over them, or just malingered under abuse and physical threat.

In theory our fifty volts gave as bright a light as the two-hundred-and-twenty volt mains of Rattleford, or the hundred and ten generated by the more respectable sets of most of our neighbours. But in practice we were rather dim, for the loss of a few volts in transit was noticeable. However, we did score by having to maintain only half the batteries of the hundred-and-ten volt people. Batteries are the most costly maintenance item of a private electric set, for the life of their plates is limited even if they are cared for reasonably. More often they are neglected until they begin to fail.

One or two people about us had dispensed with batteries, but they could only have light when the engine was running, and the traditional candle was still the middle-of-the-night stand-by. We, at least, could always have light of a sort from our batteries; quite bright immediately after a charge, but fading to a half-tone later.

One or two houses had installed magnificent diesel sets, so contrived that the engine started up on its own as soon as enough current was drawn from the batteries to put them under a load. Some of these elaborate plants would even work an electric fire.

The best-contrived set which I ever saw was a diesel plant displayed at an agricultural show. This delivered at two voltages:

two hundred and twenty for power, and fifty, through batteries, for light. It would start up on its own if any power-point were switched on within the house, and, while it was running, would charge the lighting batteries, thus giving the best of both worlds. Its owner might use standard mains power equipment, and at the same time remain unburdened by a massive block of batteries for his lights.

Yet the sets which offer the best service, even though of moderate size, cost from six to eight hundred pounds. Like all machinery, they require maintenance, overhaul, and renewals. In the end they cannot make any real approach to mains service. Lack of comprehensive rural electricity-supply is one of the first causes of the drift to the towns. The town-bred girl will not readily marry a countryman who cannot provide a servant of amperes. She has no wish to return to the conditions which had made her grandmother a matron at the age of twenty-five.

Somehow the Shallows plant has kept running. The engine turns on strangers, the dynamo flickers with long forks of imitation lightning, and the batteries are half-full of sludge. But we can still read at night, and can still pump our water up. We are coaxing the apparatus to last a few months longer before we spend money on a new, more modern plant, for there is a rumour that mains electricity may come to us and we feel that we must give the tidings the benefit of our serious doubts.

Bert Westmacott brought this news, having come upon men making a line survey while he was upon a rabbiting expedition. I wrote at once to the headquarters of the South-western area, which confirmed that the provision of mains for our scattered hamlet was indeed being considered, and added that an official of the local electricity office would call upon all us outlying people to discuss the scheme. I wrote to headquarters six months later, and received another courteous reply, which told me that they were surprised that the local official had not called, but that he would now undoubtedly write to me. It seemed to me that this promise was retrograde, but I waited for twelve months for this letter before I wrote again to headquarters. I was able now to state that I was faced in the near future with a considerable outlay for replacement of my lighting set and batteries, and that I knew of several neighbours whose plants were making such awesome noises that wives patched up any little current domestic quarrels and kissed their husbands before they allowed them to go into the engine shed. Apart from those engines which were near disintegration, the immediate neighbourhood had spent several thousand pounds on plant renewal during the course of our correspondence.

Headquarters then replied that it would cost £9000 to bring a power line to the hamlet; that they envisaged thirty-seven subscribers, of whom ten occupied large houses, eleven were farmers, and the rest cottagers. Would I be prepared to pay a line rent of £42 per annum in addition to my electricity bill? I had no idea what rent the other thirty-six prospective users were being asked, but assumed that mine was an average between cottage and large house, so that one might assume total line rent from all of us to be about £1500. This seemed a pretty good return for a capital investment of £9000, in addition to the revenue from the sale of the electricity, and I said so.

We have not had a reply to my latest letter yet, and I much fear that all we will get eventually is unfailing courtesy to counter our failing lights. It is indeed inequity that the countryman should be asked to pay so heavy a levy for being rural. And it is indeed a national error of judgment that a Parliament of urban-minded men and women should so little consider the countryman in this and many other matters.

However, none of this news was in the air during our first winter, and in those early days we rather enjoyed the diurnal feeling of achievement when we persuaded our lights to work. In any case the garden had taken possession of us, and our attention was all towards outdoors.

It seemed to us that before we could tackle the refinements we must be able to move round among the plants and shrubs. We needed a gardener less than a gang of navvies to clear the way. Bert Westmacott kept on at his ditching. He was willing enough to tend the growing things, but his only idea was to treat them with an axe.

"They old bushes want a-tearin' down."

At ditches Bert worked like a mechanical excavator. He used a

C

big shovel shaped like a jam-spoon, with a six-foot cranked handle, and the lifting of the tool was a task in itself. The canals swallowed up load after load of land-drains, and when these were laid it nearly broke Bert's heart to topple the earth back in and relay the turf, thus concealing his labours, as we hoped, for ever.

Land-drains are not designed to channel underground water-courses. Their purpose is to allow seepage through their open joints. They provide a soak-away for saturated ground, and the surplus water makes its way through the pipes to the outlet. We used the pipes only as a core for our drainage, and helped them by packing them all round with stones and rubbish to give the water additional room for filtration and to ensure that mud and gravel did not work through the pipe joints to clog the bore. When we ran out of stones and old tins we laid green brushwood along the pipes. Buried wood, left undisturbed, will last out the span of a man's life. I have often noticed, too, that acid, peaty soil, such as our moorland soil at Shallows, preserves wood.

This sort of drainage for indeterminate bogginess does not show immediate results. It is a treatment for a condition, not a specta-cular surgical operation. The water close to the pipes must find its way in to them, and when it begins to seep away the more distant moisture needs time to follow it up. But after a twelve-month we were able to walk in shoes on ground which once had sucked off knee-boots.

For the first few months we rarely saw the children. To them, at their respective ages of five and three, the garden was as vast as limbo. Now and then we came across their traces: fresh offerings of greenery, small but elaborate, appeared in the thuya clumps, where they sometimes saw fairies; long tunnels like badger runs drove deep into the heart of the huge rhododendron clumps, and at their end were magpie hoards of junk which were of great value in some land of make-believe. The children did not at first explore very far from the house, but with succeeding years their range extended. We adults too were deceived about the size of the garden, and to this day there are parts of it which we do not properly know. We can-not see the area as a whole in our mind's eye, and do not know if the reason is witchery or topography.

We were still floundering in our waterworks, happy enough among the evergreens of the garden, when our first spring burst on us. It came suddenly in a flood of colour. It was heralded but quietly by the pale, almost yellow-green, larch needles; by snow-drops and crocuses; a few white, maroon-streaked, early rhodo-dendrons; and some primulas. We had no idea that so small an advance guard would precede so tremendous an army of bloom as that which followed overnight.

The buds on the bare sticks of the azaleas, still leafless, opened quickly into flower-clusters which were six inches across. We had hardly noticed these azalea-bushes which had stood in retirement all winter like unconsidered Cinderellas. But now their groups were dressed in deep red, orange, dead white, scarlet, yellow, and in petals which combined many shades. Above them the towering rhodo-dendron banks, shaped like thirty-foot beehives, came to life. The whole visible surface of them was encrusted so thickly with flowers that the leaves were hidden. From top to ground they poured streams of many colours which hung like frozen waterfalls. Here and there taller shoots reached high up into the bare oaks, so that even these hoary old-timers seemed to have put on the trappings of youth.

The hedge which bounded us from the bridle-path to the moor was of unbroken rhododendrons, yards thick and ten-feet tall. It was no longer a hedge, but a vivid arras. Deep in the wood itself, half hidden within the oaks, birch, and hazels, a tremendous clump of scarlet rhododendrons glowed like a smouldering fire, to which chestnut boughs reached out to warm their sticky buds.

Wild hyacinths, blue, violet, and white, rose up in drifts between the uncurling shoots of fern within the wood. Primulas and then polyanthus bloomed haphazard, like daisies, in the grass. There was colour everywhere: underfoot, at eye-level, and away up among the tree-tops. Daily we discovered something new, or the children brought report of it: flowering currants; brilliant dwarf azaleas half-hidden in undergrowth; and shoals of narcissus and daffodils un-reachable through fallen timber.

Much of the pleasure was in the spendthrift nature of the display, for the best of it was not necessarily in sight of the drive or house, but in out-of-the-way corners. There were no slums in our garden, only magnificence which had sometimes become shabby. And although the spectacle was so splendid, it was shown in privacy. A holly-hedge screened it from passers-by in the lane, and traffic was infrequent, since the road came to an end on the moor a little way past our gate. The garden had dressed itself for us alone, and would have so dressed itself had no one been in the house.

The show lasted for three months, then ended as suddenly as it had begun. The garden seemed exhausted after its effort: languid as a merrymaker after a carnival. The litter of the carnival, the confetti of petals, lay ankle deep. The oaks put out their leaved arms to shade the shrubs at rest.

We too shared the exhaustion, and were glad enough to relax among the unexacting greens of the trees. However, by midsummer Tessa was saying that there were no summer flowers, that the spectacular show of spring was all very well, but that the year had three more seasons. We must, she said, find varieties of shrub and plant to follow the azaleas and rhododendrons.

It was then that we realized we could not put anything new in the garden without having to disturb it later, as slowly we cleared out the tangled dead timber, brambles, and bracken. I called Bert Westmacott away from his ditches, and we set to work with saw, axe, and bill-hook. Our place of work was marked by plumes of smoke from the bonfires, some of which burned for weeks, flaming by day, smouldering by night, in rain or shine.

CHAPTER THREE

Fire-making—The first woodpile—Firewoods—The Rhode Island Red pullets—Harry George Pengelly and the rack-saw—Converting the linhay—Cable-Street Joe—Joe and Alessandra—The return visit

THERE is a pagan instinct in me which leads me to a near-worship of fires. I am quite happy with a small one—some little smokeless effort of half a dozen twigs between a couple of flat stones. But a great, head-high pyre evokes more than happiness, and stirs deep instincts bequeathed by prehistory. Fire is the most spectacular, and possibly the most cruel, of natural elements, and when early, timid man first harnessed it to useful purposes he made perhaps his greatest single forward stride. But the relationship was never quite that between master and servant, any more than is that between a lion-tamer and his great cats, for a momentary relaxation of authority opens the door to swift and annihilating revolt. That, maybe, is why we play in fascination with the smouldering resentment of fire.

Most religions pay tacit homage to fire by allowing it a place in their ceremonies. Sometimes the practitioners save their faces by naming the flame a symbol of purity. In reality, I suspect, they accord it a place because a dim subconscious memory prompts them to propitiate the flame itself.

That first winter at Shallows Bert Westmacott and I were assiduous priests, fanning the dull embers each morning until the spirit of the fire was hungry enough to devour its daily offering. Bert, who was a bit slapdash in most things, was precise in his fire-making. I watched anxiously his first burning when we made our start on the clearance of fallen timber which tangled the feet of the tall laurels which buried the topmost linhay.

"'Tisn't possible a fellow can burn up all they rotten old branches 'less 'un tears down they rhodies," Bert remarked. He always called laurels rhodies, and rhododendrons laurels.

I wanted the laurels down, and told him to go ahead and cut they rhodies. They were the biggest laurels I had ever seen. The stems were eighteen inches thick, and, when upright, grew to forty feet or so. But some had contorted themselves and had bent almost horizontally like the bars of a living corral. Bert got at these flat ones with an axe. At the first stroke I thought we had lost his services, for the wood was so hard that the tool was deflected as if it had struck iron.

"Damn and blast 'un!" Bert exclaimed. "It do be terrible bouncey!" He applied a salivatory charm to the axe-helve, and struck again with more caution and less vigour. Quite soon a patch was covered with timber fresh-fallen over the old debris.

"Us'll burn 'un up now," Bert announced, "'less there won't be no room to work."

Now, I thought, we will see if Bert has a feeling for a fire. I saw in a moment that he had. He rummaged in his pocket for a couple of bills and a rate demand, screwed the papers into loose balls, and set them in a little clear space. He did not pick sticks off the ground, which receive the earth's dampness in all but the longest droughts, but snapped dead twigs off live trees. He selected bits no thicker than matches and laid them patiently in a tepee construction about his paper. One match started a clear flame, and an infant crackling began. He added more dead wood from the standing trees; this time pieces as thick as a finger. The flames took hold, and the heart of the little fire began to pulse with a waxing and waning blood-red glow. Its life was born, and, like a babe, it was stubborn to resist a quenching of the spark.

Now Bert added dead wood off the ground, careless of its dampness. But he was particular to snap it across his knee into even lengths of a couple of feet or so, and to lay it all in the same direction, following the course of the breeze. Presently he had cleared quite a large space of old wood.

"A chap's got room to work now," he remarked. However, like me, he did not at once take advantage of the work room, but stared at the close-knit fire.

"Folks do make a mistake laying a fire," he said. "Oftentimes they lay the sticks and trimmings athwart each other, like they was a stack of wood for seasoning. 'Tisn't a bit of good. It burns holler that-a-way. It do pay for to trim the branches clean and lay 'em all the one direction. The heap sinks down, see, as the bottom burns away to ash. The ash is fed constant, see."

My heart warmed to Bert, who had obviously given deep thought to the proper observances of kindling. Yet man is lazy, and is still as aghast as was Adam at the thought of labour. Constantly he mires his efforts in short cuts which falsely promise easement. Fires do not respond to this facile treatment: they burn holler, and the bulk of the wood remains in a scorched arch above the embers.

I do not like to fell trees—and these laurels were trees, not shrubs—but they made a tangled thicket in a space for which I had other plans. It seems always to be vandalism to destroy in a few minutes the upstanding growth of many decades. Tessa came out and caught us at our clearance. She stopped all further work until she had clambered over the whole patch to assure herself that none of our laurels were cherry laurels. Tessa is a keen experimenter with ancient formulæ, and had somewhere read that the old people used cherry-laurel leaves to simulate the flavouring of vanilla. She found none, but caused more delay by suggesting that we should strip the leaves and send them off to the wreath-makers, via Covent Garden. Bert laughed politely at first, not then knowing us well enough to say what he thought. But he threw me a desperate look when Tessa went on to say that she knew of a man who paid his rent with laurel-leaves. Finally he relaxed.

"Well, 'tisn't no manner o' use us'n picking 'un for you," he said. "You'm bought place."

Thus the laurel-leaves, the symbols of immortality which once had graced the brows of Roman heroes, were burned by Bert Westmacott. Vain human hopes of immortality have ended always in ashes and dust, yet men have continued to believe that the spirit is translated rather than destroyed. And now a school of scientific thought says, as once did the Celtic Druids, that matter is indestructible, and that it too is but transmuted when its present form is shattered. Perhaps the cycle of life and death is but a rearrangement

of atoms within a universal infinity, and our laurels have but taken
on another shape elsewhere.

Bert did not worry about all this.

"They rhodie trunks'll cut up into praaper logs for sitting-
room," he said.

We stood the massive laurel stems on end round a pine-tree, and
left them there to season a bit. This was our first wood-pile, and the
first of very many. After Bert had gone home that night Tessa and I
wandered out under the stars to kick at the loose ends fallen from the
ashes of the fire and to admire the pyramid of logs. We thought
we saw half a winter's burning in our pile, but a log-heap teaches the
converse of the saying that the eye is often larger than the stomach.
Here the belly of the grate is larger than the store of fuel, and the
largest pile melts into the flames too quickly.

We were unused to burning wood, and nothing but wood, in a
grate. We knew coal, and we knew peat, but wood exclusively was
a fresh experience. Except for the kitchen, with its cook-and-heat,
all the rooms in Shallows had grates. The grates were standard
types, each with an iron basket in which the coals were meant to
burn. We tried at first to burn our wood in the baskets, and had
indifferent success. Then I tried with the baskets out, lighting the
fires on the hearthstone itself, just as our distant ancestors had done.
Now the logs were able to lie on a bed of their own ash, and their
heating quality was transformed. The ash bed itself became a
reservoir of warmth, and of a morning some log remnant was always
aglow on its underside, ready to flame up at the breath of the
bellows.

Wood may be used to eke out coals, but the converse should
never be attempted. If wood is the predominant fuel it must be
used alone, or possibly with peat. The clinker and the ash of even
a few coals destroy the purity of a wood fire.

Shallows became an exacting mistress. The place demanded
always our attention. When we came to use our first wood-pile of
laurels we did not lay the logs in the hearth anonymously, but were
reminded at once of the corner from which they had come. I had
wanted to clear up a lot of writing that night of the first wood fire,
but Tessa, seated on the floor watching the spreading flame, said that

it was nice to be able to get to the top linhay now that the laurels were cleared.

We began to talk of the linhay's future. Should we adapt it for fowls, or a pig, or both? Would the cleared ground make a run, or lawn, or an orchard? Thus it always was on a winter's night by the firelight. The wide variety of logs gave their reminders of an equal variety of problems in as many corners of the garden. Sometimes oak logs, sawn from fallen boughs dragged through the brambles of the wood, reminded us of lacerated flesh, and urged on us the need to tackle that wilderness. Sometimes holly prompted us to plan a topping of the holly-hedge along the lane. Rhododendron wood gave us a quiet nudge to set about clearing the dead branches which choked the interior of the great evergreen banks. We burned ash, pine, cypress, larch, sycamore, fir, beech, birch, and even alder and elder. Each and every one of them intruded upon our evenings. Tessa, staring into the fire-glow from her place on the floor, would presently say:

"I heard somewhere that beech won't rot in water. I wonder if we ought to have kept this to revet that soft bank in the fish-pond."

Or:

"I wish you wouldn't cut down all the elder-trees. I want to make some wine. And I've found an old recipe for elder-flower water for the complexion."

I would put down my pen and go over to the fire to give earnest attention to whatever sort of wood glowed there. We would begin to make plans for the fish-pond, and, leading from that watery premise, for improving the run of the streams, cleaning out the silted lily-pond, draining a bog in the wood, and the growing of water-cress. Or else we would drift imperceptibly from elderberries to parsnip wine, sloe gin, and other militant concoctions of the gentle countryside. As often as not some bold idea would strike us, and out we would go into the night to reconnoitre its translation into fact. Like a Delilah, Shallows wooed me from my purpose on most evenings. I knew that I was being infirm, but could not resent the enticement which made me so.

All this sitting and staring of a night at least made us fine judges of the calorific values of the different woods. Quite soon we learned to blend our fuel; to restrain the exuberance of pine, holly, or ash, with the dignity of oak and the dullness of laurel and rhododendron. Oak may be a fine wood to put on with coals, but burned alone in a pure wood fire it is slow to rouse. However, when well aglow its heat is intense, and its embers have great endurance.

It parallels the Anglo-Saxon character, for which it is so often held up as a symbol.

The softwoods made us a little nervous, for their firework display of sparks was unsuited to a house so largely built of boarding, so we quickly learned to adapt our wood to our movements. Whenever the garden allowed us to settle down in the sitting-room we would drop a few pine logs on to the embers to enjoy an immediate blaze; when we wished the fire safely to maintain a good heat in our absence, we stacked it with sober oak, laurel, or rhododendron.

The brooding over the laurel logs of our first wood-pile did in fact lead to action at the top linhay. We made up our minds to keep some hens in it. Bert Westmacott thought the plan correct, saying that 'twas a praaper shame for to buy stale old Government eggs from they robbers in Rattleford, when us could grow 'un from our own fowls.

The linhay had a pitched roof, but was open on one side, and the floor was earth. Obviously I was going to need a good deal of wood to cover the floor—for hens hate damp—and to board in the open side. Here, at once, we came up against the constant economic problem of the smallholder. Firstly, there was the capital cost of the labour to convert the linhay, and to make a wire run. Secondly, there was the labour of looking after the hens: the work would be little enough, but it was worth at least a few pence a day. I was secretly convinced that we could buy our eggs cheaper than we could produce them. However, Bert was determined to pretend that Shallows was a gentleman's residence, and that as such it should be supported by the nearest to a home-farm that he could contrive; Tessa saw herself in well-cut dungarees, gathering rich brown eggs into a basket; and the children, who had got wind of the scheme, insisted that we went through with it.

Louise by this time had become a great roamer, and within a

day or two of learning the plan came home to say that she had located a dozen Rhode Island Red pullets, and said that I could have them provided they were removed at once from the vendor. We were not ready to receive the birds, but every one, led by Bert, beseeched me to fetch 'un quick, being as they was so handy. I did so, paying heavily for the privilege, and turned them loose in the dog-kennel linhay, with free range in the garden until their permanent quarters were prepared.

It was extraordinary how the introduction of this corporate entity of twelve auburn birds disrupted the life of our family. Tessa, who had sown several varieties of seed, neglected meals and mending to protect her flowers and vegetables. The children apostrophized her for hurling clods at the trespassers, and enticed them into the protection of their nursery, with its convenient door on to the veranda. Bert left all his urgent work to put up the run, and badgered me from morning to night to get him some timber to convert the linhay. The children tried to dissuade me from immuring their new pets. We all became bad-tempered except the Rhodes, who seemed very happy among the seeds and seedlings.

Exhorted by all, except the children and chickens, I began to cast around for some timber. After a few days I had to report to Bert that the prospect was bleak; that a large proportion of the machinery of centralized government had been set up in the district to thwart me; that I had, however, promises from a few of the more bucaneering timber men, and something might therefore turn up one day. Bert must have been aware of my ignorance of the West Country character.

"Aye?" he exclaimed, in the tone which goes with expectoration. "Them'll promise t'clothes off back to be rid of 'ee if 'ee worries 'em for summat as'll give 'em a bit of work. Beats me how 'un all lives, bein' so tired from birth. Don't 'ee reckon nowt to promises 'bout these parts."

With the appearance of a man who wants to be fair, he added:

"'Tisn't as if 'un was all liars, mind. 'Tis just as 'un can't tell truth, like."

As so often happens, however, the solution of the problem lay within a stone's throw, where a gnome lived in conjunction with water sprites. The gnome was ostensibly a farmer named Harry George Pengelly, who inhabited Blackaton Farm on the fringe of our scattered hamlet of a dozen dwellings. Harry George was a little spry man of whom, in those early days, I had caught only glimpses. Several times I had briefly seen his agile small figure flit across the lane, capped by a tight navy beret, and carrying a long hazel stick like a wand. But always the brisk, neat form vanished from under my very eye before I could even so much as bid him good-day.

But one morning during the hen and timber trouble I was walking deep in thought past Blackaton, when Harry George materialized in front of me within touching distance. He fixed me with his bright fey eyes and said that if I was wanting for timber why ever didn't I send along some of my own sticks to be cut up on his rack-saw. He told me the dimensions and number of planks I would need for the linhay, and enumerated such of the various felled trees which were lying about Shallows which would give the required footage. I supposed to myself that he had slid along a moonbeam some night recently to investigate the goings-on of his new neighbours.

However, I expressed aloud great interest in the rack-saw, whereupon Harry George whisked me through a gate into a field where an open tin shed leaned against a long farm building whose roof-tree wandered about at all levels and angles like the Great Wall of China. At one point the eaves drooped to within a few feet of the ground, and a young wether had sprung up on to the slates to eat the herbage which sprouted between their joints.

The rack-saw lay in the open shed, spanning a pit filled with sawdust which gave off a fragrance of resin. The plant was driven from a contrivance of overhead shafting which could only have been devised by a mechanically minded pixie. The pulleys were all of wood, deeply grooved by the run of the belting. Long wooden levers, roughly hand-trimmed, hung from the shafting, and, by some principle of leverage whose formula was long lost to engineering, acted as tensioners. In some way each brought into action a different belt, each belt being driven by a pulley of a different diameter. Thus a form of gearing was available to the operator.

I thought, as I tried to fathom the system, that Harry George could have done it all much more quickly by casting a spell.

Harry George was delighted at my interest. He explained that water-power drove his machinery, and that his leat ran for a couple of miles up to the source of the Teign. In the 1930's Torquay Corporation had dammed the headwaters to form a huge reservoir to ensure that their citizens might not have to go either thirsty or unwashed, except voluntarily. The great scheme, however, had been planned around Harry George's water easement, for no one in the land might deny the flow to the leat. Had anyone done so, there is no doubt that Harry George would have caused dragons to twist and turn uneasily beneath the foundations of the dam, so that the whole cast structure would have cracked and sunk, as did once the walls of King Vortigern's castle.

Nothing would do but that I must pay my respects to the water. Harry George vanished through a crevice in the stone wall of the building against which the tin shed was propped. To my mild surprise my bulk was instantly adjusted to squeeze after him, as he bobbed away ahead of me, sinking deeper and deeper below the earth. Here and there an electric bulb showed dimly enough to point the darkness. A dynamo hummed somewhere with the sonic depth of a beehive, and as background music was the steady rush of water, angry at confinement. These themes were punctuated by the spin of shafting in its bearings, and the flick-flick of many driving belts of unknown purposes.

Harry George was darting all over the place to play tunes on his machinery, then to take me by the elbow while he explained what task each contrivance would perform when coaxed. I am sure that none would have so performed for anyone else. The experience was eerie to a degree, and when I thought about it later I was half persuaded that I had once seen Harry George flittering along a moving belt, and running round a spinning pulley.

At any rate, by established accord with my neighbour, enough felled trees were fetched from Shallows, sawn, and returned, to do the work so earnestly desired. Only one happening caused me to wonder whether Harry George Pengelly had pixilated the enterprise. I had got Bert to build a broad platform within the linhay rather than to lay a wood floor over the whole interior. The platform was supported on stout uprights of laurel taken from our wood-pile, still unconsumed by the sitting-room fire. The wood was now well-seasoned, and was so hard that we thought it would last out a lifetime, even though an end of each support was to be buried in the earth. It did better than offer passive resistance to rot. Some months later I chanced to stoop and peer under the platform. The laurel posts had sprouted leaved branches as prolifically as in the days of the original jungle, and I foresaw the linhay as a tree-top eyrie, lifted to the height of a tall ladder.

However, it was one thing to provide a home for the Rhodes; it was quite another to make them live in it. The birds had become used to a carefree life among the seeds and young growing plants, and would not lightly forego the old spacious ways. They showed a diabolical ingenuity in escaping from their confinement, and had they laid an egg a day apiece for the term of their adult lives, they could never have repaid the cost of the man-hours spent in hunting them down. In the end we got the better of them all, except one blowsy hen whom the children had named Primrose. Primrose defeated us. Clipped wings did not hold her, nor, I believe, would gyves have done. Worse still, she was in full lay, and search as we would, we could not discover her nest.

I ought to have become suspicious at the half-hearted help of the children as we sought the increasing clutch of Primrose's eggs, for they had formerly been keen enough to hunt stray nests. One morning I happened to enter their bedroom before they were up. The two of them were in one bed, and between them sat Primrose, making dust-bath motions. The door of the wardrobe had been opened and in a corner I caught a glimpse of eggs making a fine clutch in a nest of old clothes.

Primrose remained a favourite of the children, and when a couple of years later we began to eat the dozen original Rhodes we left her until the last, producing her as an anonymous fowl at table without comment. To our relief the children ate with their usual gusto. After a second helping it became apparent that they had not been deceived, for at the end Louise said loyally: "I think Primrose tasted the most delicious of them all."

In the days when the Rhodes were still alive to pester us, one or other would sometimes go broody. The children used then, surreptitiously, to push a clutch of eggs under the maternally minded bird. Tessa was the first to discover this gracious little gesture, and I noticed her with her two daughters in earnest explanation of the necessity to use fertile eggs for such a purpose.

A few days later I began to see frequently in our garden a Light Sussex cockerel which belonged to old Robertson at Westhill. The bird was a sturdy flyer, and found no difficulty in soaring over the netting which enclosed the Rhodes. I did not realize that his visits were due to other than his male avian instincts, until I discovered one day that a trail of corn was being laid from Westhill to us. I did not relish the idea of our daughters acting as procuresses, and decided to buy some day-old chicks to slip under the next broody. At that time I was often in a market-town on the other side of the moor and had noticed several stallholders who sold day-olds.

The next time that Bert came along to say that one of they old fowls was broody, and should he hang 'un up in a sack to bring 'un to her senses, I told him to let 'un bide as 'un was, because I was going to get some titchy chicks.

It was thus that I met Cable Street Joe. He was a little, respectable-seeming man, with bushy hair flushed back in two bow-waves from a wide brow. His eyes were as bright and quick as those of the chicks he sold. His wife was with him: a plump, dark Italian woman, twice his size, dressed in heavy black. She would have been one of the crowd in a South European town, but was to be remarked in the Devon moorland market where I found them behind a stall.

At that first encounter Cable Street Joe had but one box left of a dozen day-olds. I said that I would have them, but would call for them later. When at length I returned, paid up, and took the box, I saw Joe give his wife a satisfied look. It was so marked, and so clearly connected with my purchase, that I asked the reason.

"Like this, see!" said Joe in a quick Cockney accent, most out of place in that sleeping town. "Missus ses I didn't ought to've kept the chicks for you. Could've sold 'em dozen times over. How do we know 'e's comin' back? Why couldn't 'e've took 'em first time? What's 'is lark? You never heard so many questions. 'E'll be back, I ses. 'E'll be back. It's in 'is face."

I wondered aloud how my fate was so importantly bound up with the chickens that the mark of our relationship was set on my fore-head.

"'Tisn't nothing to do with the day-olds," said Joe. "Said you was 'aving them, didn't you? Back you've come, 'aven't you? Straight 'e is, I ses to the missus. Them few chickens isn't worth a gent like 'im doin' the dirty over."

I suppose it was a kind of compliment.

I took the chicks back with me, and that night, when the broody hen was dozing in her coop in the darkness, Tessa and I took them out of the airing cupboard and slipped them one by one beneath her wings.

At first light the children reported that all twelve babies were well, and that Marigold, the mother, was pleased with herself, not know-ing any better.

I can never work up much enthusiasm over birds hatched and reared in a succession of mechanical contrivances. The process is in-human, whatever its economic value. There is a taint of immorality in the therapeutic when it is applied to reproduction, which the carnal escapes.

We bought more boxes of chicks from time to time, always now from Joe, and gradually I came to know a little about him from our chats in the market. I learned, for instance, that he lived in Ply-mouth, though until he approached middle age his life had been spent in Bethnal Green. I learned that he had been in the Army during the recent German war, and that he had enlisted willingly. Unfortunately he had been posted to one of those badly commanded units which are uncommon, but not unknown, in the British Forces. As a consequence he became afflicted with the military disease of bloody-mindedness, and had determined to return to civilian life. He wished to obtain his release through the proper channels, and had therefore feigned a feebleness of intellect, with various neurotic subsidiary symptoms. This had proved to be a ticket for the booths of the psychiatrists, whom he had been at pains to furnish with much text-book material. In the end he had been passed on to a most superior being who had power to order release.

Here Joe surpassed himself. Unfortunately his symptoms became so unusual and interesting that the psychiatrist was loath to let go of him, or alternatively wished to incarcerate him in a mental home where he would be available for inspection, like a specimen in a bottle. Joe had to lapse into a lucid interval in order to suggest that his wife might be sent for in order to lead him home. To his relief this was decided upon, and the Army lost, on grounds of stupidity, a recruit who might well have graced higher staffs as a master of deception and the cover plan.

This slice of Joe's history we learned when we visited him in Plymouth at his invitation. Joe and his wife Alessandra, with their two beautifully mannered young daughters, lived in a room above a ground-floor apartment which housed nothing but incubators and boxes filled with newly hatched chicks. Throughout our stay a multitudinous chirruping pervaded the little, narrow house, and we were comforted by the warm, cosy smell peculiar to a quantity of artificially reared chicks. We drank pots of strong tea, and ate, of all things, mounds of smoked-salmon sandwiches. Joe and Alessandra did not care for smoked salmon, and Tessa and I were happy to avoid giving offence by eating the lot.

At our departing Alessandra descended somehow the steep and twisting stair, and thrust into Tessa's lap, as she settled herself in the car, a packet of sugar and a pound of margarine.

It was azalea time in our second year at Shallows, when Joe and his wife paid their return visit to us. We sat on the veranda under the broad, budding spread of the wistaria, and looked across the stream which always danced more lightly in the sunshine, across the crimson-splashed wall of rhododendrons beside the bridle-path, and on to the billowing moor due south of us. Alessandra, in heavy black, almost purred in the heat which had driven Tessa and me into shorts. Louise and Johanna were capering naked in and out of the water.

Joe's alert eye noticed some books on a table, of which one was a crime thriller.

"Started to read that, the other day," he said. "Had to throw it away. Threw it away, true as I'm sitting here. Didn't I, Mother?"

Alessandra assented sleepily and amiably.

I asked how the book had offended.

D

"Remember where they coshed the bloke at the races? Crowned him with a bit of piping and run off into the crowd? It's not done like that!" asserted Joe indignantly.

I expressed interest.

"Not a bit of it," went on Joe, with the animation of a man who relives great days. "You don't bash a bloke and run. You want to give him a proper doing, don't you? So you want to take him away with you some place quiet, don't you?"

I agreed that this seemed the proper course.

"Certainly it is!" Joe exclaimed heartily. "What you does is two of you goes up on each side. You've got your bit of piping in a rolled-up newspaper, haven't you? All neat and tidy so no one won't take offence. You cosh him, and as his knees give each of you takes an arm. You both act a bit drunk, but not as drunk as him. You're helping your pal, see? You can walk him past a couple of coppers easy as pie, provided you wink at 'em cheerful like. Many's the chap as 'as been done that way, and no one a bit put out."

I said that it all seemed to be a question of good manners. There was a right way to do everything.

Joe remarked to Tessa that you could always tell an educated bloke by the way he caught on. So appreciative an audience warmed his spirit, tapped his memory, and loosened a tongue which was naturally guarded. It was at first difficult to know whether the information we gained was at second hand via Joe the observer, or at first hand from Joe the man of action. But slowly 'what a pal of mine done' gave way to 'what I done.'

The way of life in Cable Street and its neighbourhood was un-expected in some ways. For instance, the gangs, according to Joe, did not frequent the public houses so much as the cafés and little restaurants. It was in one or another of these that they usually made their respective headquarters. The battles of their internecine war-fare were usually arranged meetings, as formal as the solemn mutual approach march and attack of armies in the days of chivalry. But in Bethnal Green the weapons were mostly jagged bottles and steel-shod boots.

The police very sensibly let these affairs run their course, but the participants relied on the officers to take care of casualties. These

unfortunates were always laid out in rows under neutral arrangements in a yard which adjoined some tenements known as The
Buildings, and were picked up by the police on receipt of a telephone call.

We humans so readily take for granted the conveniences of our
environment. There was an occasion when Joe muscled in on some
West End territory. It was not until he and his assistants stood
bloody but victorious among the prostrate figures on the battle-
ground that they realized that up West there was, so far as they knew,
no equivalent of The Buildings. They were as much at a loss as
would be a fighting battalion without access to a Casualty Clearing
Station. I do not believe that this foreign venture of Joe's was of
long duration, and I have felt that one and all were glad to return
to the haunts they knew, and to have once again at hand the great
convenience of The Buildings.

We sat that warm, golden spring afternoon, Joe and Alessandra,
Tessa and I, breathed upon by the scented airs of the garden, our
eyes lighting unconfined on the distant moorland skyline, our ears
musicked by nothing but birdsong and the theme of running streams.
Joe and Alessandra were happy, and perhaps did not know why.
Tessa and I were happy, and the more so as the contrast was
pointed between our garden and the scene of Joe's tales.

He came to tell of the poverty which is so much the more bitter
in the sterile places of brick and pavement, which are even yet un-
natural for man, so recently a pastoral animal. He told of the petty
crime which was the destined career of many youths, since they were
fitted for nothing else, and were set no other example in the ant-
heap of the slums.

Joe's description of the love-making seemed fantastically unreal,
but only, perhaps, because at Shallows the sordid smear was so difficult to see in the imagination. The love-making began in the very
early teens, and was consummated, often enough, in the standing
room at the back of the cinemas. If not there, at least the most
extensive preliminaries were carried out, and were later brought to
a conclusion on the concrete stairways or corridors of the blocks
of tenements.

At the cinemas the young humans were less selective than many animal species. There was a brief pressing together in the darkness, a rebuff or an acquiescence from the dimly seen stranger; a press against the next figure in the darkness, or a mating without passing on.

We asked why Joe had left the jungle of bricks and pavements of which he had been a denizen; and, if he had left because he was sickened of towns, why then had he made his new lair in a smaller jungle of similar composition.

There was no clear answer. Perhaps there were reasons connected with the ferocity of the other animals in his native parts; or with the hunters, the police. At any rate, he made it clear that he could not bear to live out in the countryside of fields, mountains, hedges, and woods. He was as uncomfortable there as would be any species of the animal world transported to a habitat alien to its habits. He was not allergic to the countryside, however, as were so many wartime evacuees, for instance. He enjoyed the flavour of it, provided he could taste it in his native environment. Thus he was happy in his little Plymouth house, looking out on busy streets and smoking chimneys, with his chicken hatchery on the ground floor.

He was delighted when we filled the back of his car with cut azaleas of many brilliant and subtle colours to turn his tiny square sitting-room into a cave of Aladdin. He even asked shyly whether we ever heard of a kitten for sale. He thought that every home should have a cat.

Tessa was gone in a flash, and returned with a two-months old female, incredulous to the last that anyone would wish for it. A female cat is as unwanted among rustics as is a girl-child among Chinese peasants. Both infants are likely to die the death before they are conscious of life.

As Joe drove away that afternoon in a respectable, upright Austin, Alessandra handed Tessa a box of eggs out of the car window, and Joe accelerated to leave protest behind. The last we saw of the venerable box-like vehicle was the glow of our azaleas in the back. With Alessandra dressed in heavy black, the outfit would have passed for a hearse with well-wreathed coffin. The two of them returned to the town, but somewhere in their subliminal minds stirred the memory of the cleaner country days of our kind. Tessa and I pictured their cell of a room that night, cosy with the wafted heat of chickens, warmed with the colour of the azaleas, and a kitten on the plush arm-chair. Not even Bethnal Green can kill the old instincts.

CHAPTER FOUR

Pandy—The essentials of a gentleman's residence—Meadow into lawn: turfing and draining—The Topgoods and The Machine —The consequences of making a lawn—Defence against birds

Tᴇssᴀ's alacrity in disposing of a female kitten was no quicker than that which a neighbour had shown in bestowing the female kitten's mother on us. It had happened that Louise's birthday had fallen due within a few days of our ingoing at Shallows. We knew no children to form even a skeleton party, but had heard unmistakable juvenile sounds in the garden and fields of a house a furlong or two away. We telephoned to beg the use of a few children to share the cakes and crackers of a birthday tea. The strange children attended, and brought with them a present which became the success of the day. This was a half-grown, nondescript tabby female named Pandy. Pandy was probably the least eligible gift cat within the boundaries of Dartmoor Forest.

Nevertheless, she made her home with us with the thick-skinned persistence of a feline. The children adored her, though Tessa and I, who both like cats, could not pretend to a great affection for this one. She was from the first a barefaced thief, and unrepentant. With all the wilderness of garden at her disposal, and living in a house whose walls were no more than a string of exits, she preferred to perform her necessary but unattractive eliminatory duties within doors. I would cheerfully have performed an eliminatory duty upon her with a rifle, but that she and the children were inseparable and that Shallows inhibited my urge to kill.

In return for a lease of life which was more precarious than she knew, Pandy repaid in two ways. She became a very good hunter; and she taught the children the processes of courtship, mating, birth, suckling, and weaning.

A female cat is a better hunter than the male, because she is but briefly preoccupied with sex, though at rather frequent intervals. The tom-cat, however, has no intervals whatever in his preoccupation. If he hunts at all it is only because he bumps into a quarry while he is moving from one serenade to the next. Following from this, it is almost certain that what vermin he does kill are on other people's ground, leaving mice and voles and rats to swarm about his own home.

But the female hunts at home. She does not have to leave her boundaries to seek a tom when the fancy takes her, for a dozen rivals are on hand before the female is even sure in her own mind that she is again stirred by the rhythm which moves every living thing in its particular orbit of rest, activity, feeding, and reproduction. The she-cat will continue to hunt until the hour of confinement, and will recommence within the week with the more vigour and ferocity now that her young are laid by in her den.

Pandy, for instance, never troubled to kill rabbits except when she had a growing litter. Usually she killed for sport only: mice, voles, rats, and moles. But when her kittens were mewling about in their traditional nursery below the hot-water cylinder she often brought rabbits into them. She was also a cat in the old tradition, not believing that the young should be brought up to expect manna from a Welfare State. As soon as the eyes of her litter had been open long enough to focus she would introduce live mice to the airing cupboard, teaching her children how to practise hypnosis, how to feint and parry with a quarry; and how to extract the utmost, lingering pleasure from torture and death. Pandy taught her young early the cruelty of the natural world where quarter is neither given nor expected. Yet perhaps there is no cruelty in nature, since mercy is not known to any plant and to no animal save a proportion of the human species. Cruelty is not the quality which obtrudes in nature, for it is woven into the fabric of life. It is mercy, the new idea cooked up half-heartedly by man, which in its artificiality disturbs the pattern of the ages.

If Louise and Johanna learned that lesser animals lived by ruthlessness, they learned too the cleanliness of the natural sex impulse. They saw the train of events which bent to form the cycle of life, and quickly associated each with its consequence.

There was only room for one child's head in the airing cupboard, and during Pandy's accouchements the child in front would give a running commentary to the other. Much hinged on the order of birth, since Pandy's litters were always variegated, and the children had a marked colour preference, both preferring ginger. Thus when they noticed by Pandy's bulk, and by the development of what they called her "milkers," that confinement was near, they would decide in advance which kitten in order of birth would belong to whom.

The unsighted child would writhe in an agony of frustration as the other called out in the style of a sports broadcaster that number one was tabby, but that the second had a black head, and with any luck would bear white markings. Yes! No! Yes! It had indeed a white tummy. As for the third, her money was on ginger this time.

Indeed, between hens, rabbits, and Pandy at home, assisted by the beasts of the field who dwelt without the garden, the children learned the lessons of life with simplicity and cleanliness. It was not until they came of an age to cultivate their own gardens that we realized how much less comprehensible are the fertilizing methods and reproductive systems of plants.

One day I overheard Tessa and Louise by the melon frame. The child was very proud of the large number of yellow flowers on the sprawling stems, until Tessa explained that most of the blossoms were male. The two of them put their heads together in that way women have when they are forming a coven to say something derogatory about the useless sex. Sure enough, Tessa explained that the male of any species was really pretty useless, being unable to reproduce his kind. The male melon-flower conformed to type, being an idle ornament. She did concede, however, that its pollen must be introduced to the female flower so that it might bear fruit, and she showed Louise how to perform the introduction with a feather.

The child bent busily over the plant, silent in thought as she worked, until after a while she remarked how much more simple it was for Pandy and Major, the Westhill tom.

While the local fauna were educating our children Bert Westmacott was trying to educate me in the essentials of a gentleman's residence. The essentials were lawns, driveways, and flower-beds. Over coffee of a morning Bert insinuated his propaganda, week after week. We heard of the noble houses where he had been groom; of greenswards as big as all Harry George Pengelly's farm; private drives which would have reached the two miles to Rattleford; and flower-beds big as mangle fields, full of they tulips.

I resisted persuasion for a while. I thought that the place would look tidy enough if the shrubberies were cleared of debris; the long grass scythed; low branches lopped; and the walls and rockeries weeded. I was wrong, and was puzzled what action to take that was within my resources.

It came to me that Bert was as right in his three essentials of lawns, drives, and flower-beds as was Field-Marshal Montgomery in his eight points of war. It was true that the old stately homes employed a legion of gardeners in their battle against untidiness, but then they were fighting on a vast front of parks, lakes, private playing-fields, tennis courts, rose gardens, greenhouses, topiary work, and yew-hedges. The forces available were no more than adequate for their commitments. I realized that my private army of Bert was just as adequate for my own narrow front.

These casual-seeming country gentry of the past generation were, of course, anything but haphazard in their domestic methods indoors and out. The lady of the house was the scourge of kitchen and still-room. She was trained from infancy in the complexities of running a great establishment without waste. Just so were the menfolk trained in outdoor matters, and the training was reinforced by several centuries of instinctive know-how. Bert's lawns, drives, and beds had not come by accident, but had evolved because they were the factors without which in proper condition nothing else availed. If they were well-kept, other deficiencies were obscured. Most important of all, they were very easily and cheaply kept once they were laid out.

Tessa and I capitulated. One day, when Bert said was it up among they old brimbles in the wood we wanted him to go slashing to-day, I delighted him by saying that we were going to make the meadow into a lawn. We all trooped out and spent a happy half-hour looking at the piece of ground, making heel-marks to see where the damp bits were, and prodding sticks into it to locate rocks. The construction of a garden, as distinct from its maintenance, is peculiar in that one views imminent hard labour with pleasure. In this case the hard labour was well in view.

The meadow was that piece of rough grass on which Tessa had stood on our first visit in order to ask just where the meadow was. Its area was about a fifth of an acre. It sloped irregularly from the two largest rhododendron clumps to the drive, with a difference of perhaps five feet between top and bottom levels. Two large apple-trees grew in one corner and were obviously immovable, but half a dozen much younger trees were of a size to transplant. There was an open ditch through the middle which carried a trickle of water which had no visible source. The entire surface mat was of couch-grass, ground elder, docks, and thistles.

"'Twill surely make a praaper job of a lawn," said Bert uncertainly at the end of our reconnaissance. And, indeed, when I looked at the wheelbarrow, which rested idly on the drive with pick and spade lying asleep in it, I too felt uncertain. It was all very well for the Assyrians to plan their vast city mounds with no implements in sight except the growing materials to weave carrying baskets. But they were able to turn twenty or thirty thousand expendable slaves on to the job. We had only one Bert, who was not expendable, and who was beginning to wipe his mouth thirstily on the back of his hand at the very thought of what was to be done.

"Us must root up they young trees, then skim off turf," said Bert resolutely.

At once we were faced with the recurrent problem at Shallows: what did we do with they trees when they were rooted up and the turf when 'twas skum? The problem did not recur in the same form, but the poser was always similar. If we wished to clear rocks, we must build a rockery to absorb them. If we wished to dig out a bog to form a pool, we must find a hollow to level with the bog spoil. If we wished to relieve a shrubbery of half a hundred sturdy suckers, we must decide what part of the wood to clear ready to take them.

We were forced to accept the theory that matter was indestructible. At Shallows it was but transposed.

Tessa adopted the air of a *chatelaine*, and said that she would like to begin a proper orchard up by the top linhay in the space where Bert had massacred the laurels. The ground there, so long dank and shadowed, was still grassless. Let the turf be relaid there, and the young fruit-trees transplanted. Having uttered this fiat in the airy manner of Genesis, Tessa drifted away. I, thank goodness, also had business elsewhere. Bert said he was going off home to fetch his turfing iron. He said it in the weighty manner of a Horatius Cocles asking some one to keep an eye on the bridge while he got his sword.

Bert spat on his hands for several days, plied his turfing iron, which had his favourite long and cumbersome type of cranked handle, then came to announce that the meadow was skum. I could see that he had enjoyed every moment of his appalling labour. We have built machines with brains: when we can also endow them with souls, Bert may perhaps be reincarnated as a bulldozer.

The naked meadow was now fortified by walls of turves dotted here and there like early British breastworks, and before we might move them Tessa pointed out that their new homes must undergo preparation, for the old laurel ground was all humps and hollows and was liable to periodic flooding. We soon levelled the humps into the hollows, but the flooding was not easily controlled, for all the vast Shallows waterworks were at the extreme other boundary of the garden. The flooding came from a stream far above us which periodically came to visit across a lane and three rough fields. The only way at our disposal to control it was to dig a perimeter dyke round the two sides of the property.

I was beginning to be afraid of the magnitude of the task which we had undertaken, but told myself that the ditch was necessary, apart from its distant relationship with the lawn. However, I was puzzled when I saw Bert arrive at work with hedging gloves and a bill-hook.

"'Tisn't possible a man can get at ditch 'less 'un trims they old hedges," he pointed out indignantly. "They h'aint been touched for ye'rs and ye'rs, m'dear."

So Bert vanished from sight for a week among thick hazels, ash, and rowan, brimbles, and what he called docks and doysels. Bonfires marked his progress to the bitter and sanguinary end, and every now and again Tessa would walk out with a bucket and hand-shovel to collect the ash to put on the newly bared earth of the former meadow in an arc about the foot of the two great rhododendron clumps.

We finished the ditch at last, running it into the nearer stream; we laid the turves by the top linhay on the mould formed by generations of shed laurel-leaves; and we spaced therein the young fruit-trees uplifted from the meadow. The meadow now became the embryo lawn.

I stood on the hard earth one morning with Bert. I was telling him that we must fork it over; break up the clods of packed soil; rake the tilth smooth; and sow it with grass seed. Bert was mentally spitting on both hands when Tessa wandered out to ask what we proposed now. I repeated the programme. She left us, to make measured paces longways and sideways, then to remark that there was comfortable room to level a badminton court without running into the two mature apple-trees we had had to leave *in situ*. Bert and I looked at one another in panic. The indomitable human spirit, sprung from no definable source, prompted me to follow her paces, and, sure enough, room there was. However, the agile human brain prompted me to say at once that I played my badminton at night, under cover, in the village hall.

Tessa exposed male egotism by saying that, yes, dear, but the children were nearly ready to handle rackets, and could not be expected to remain in Rattleford until the inns closed during the indoor badminton season. Bert and I looked at the slope of the bared meadow, and at its open ditch. Finally I sent him off to slash at they brimbles in the wood while I thought about this new problem which had now been removed from the horticultural to the domestic.

There was a period of outward quietude, during which I frequently assured Tessa that I was just considering how best to proceed, and that there were some intricate problems of logistics to be worked out. She remarked daily, as if apropos of nothing, on the forcing nature of the warm and humid Devon climate, and the lushness of growth which it promoted. For example, even the skum meadow bade fair to be green again in a few weeks with a fresh crop of couch, ground ivy, docks, and doysels. Nature, she thought, was wonderful to repair Bert's ravages so rapidly.

The fact was that I funked the levelling. I had worked out with much labour the entire content of soil to be lifted from the high end in order to build up the low. I foresaw that by Bert and barrow there was a summer's work. The open ditch would be so deep below the new surface that obviously it must be piped and covered over, yet I could not be sure that it would then remain effective, for none of us could discover whence came the water which filtered into it. Also there were the ponderous imponderables of several boulders at the high end, now flush with the soil, which would protrude when that part was lowered and which we might or might not be able to move.

During this stalemate Tessa advised me one day that she had asked some people to lunch. The Topgoods were a young colonel of the disbanded Indian Army and his wife. Rattleford had proved to be a repository of the dispossessed, and we had by now a chatting aquaintance with Anglo-Indian political agents and soldiers; with tea-planters; with British naval, Army, and Air Force folk; and with former landed gentry; all of whom had moved into the Rattleford district to be among their kind, and to form a bastion against the flood of social disintegration.

The Topgoods were rather smart. I could picture them a-stroll in the formal gardens of yesteryear; and sitting on the balustraded terrace to await the butler with the preprandial decanters. Instead we could show them little except the devasted meadow, since they were not equipped to traverse bog and brimble; and, that shown, and sympathy extracted, we sat them on the veranda to drink sherry. We sat them on the veranda again after lunch to drink coffee. The colonel said very little, huddled into a chair as if he was chilly. The wife chattered of nothing, as was the social custom of the olden times, ten years before.

When our guests had gone Tessa and I thought that the visit had not been a success. We both loved Shallows, but we were not so blind as to believe that strangers also must love at sight the ramshackle conglomeration of clapboard and tin which was the house, nor see with the futurist's eye the pools and bog-gardens, and, indeed, velvet lawns which our own vision superimposed on morasses and weed-grown earth.

We were surprised therefore when the Topgoods telephoned an invitation in return, the more so since they hesitantly asked if we would bring them a cutting of wistaria.

They lived in a real house of stone, with parquet floors, which stood graciously in a real garden. We wondered briefly what our hosts had thought of our own rude log hut on its native moorland shelf; briefly, because we were hurried through the rooms to a glass door, through which we were ushered. We found ourselves, a little bewildered, on a veranda very like our own, save that it was new and had nice clean paintwork.

Our hosts began to explain, both at once. We must have thought them rather unforthcoming the other day. The fact was that they had been transported in mind back to India; back to creeper-shaded verandas—had we brought the wistaria cutting?—and had not so enjoyed a visit for a long time. As we could see, they had at once begun to build a veranda similar to ours. It had only been finished for a few days, and now they spent most of their time there.

The wistaria cutting was taken from us, and lunch grew cold while alternative positions for its planting were argued. Tessa and I were delighted that even hard-cased Anglo-Indians were not immune from the spell of Shallows, for we always felt about the place as does a lover introducing his beloved for the first time. He wishes her to scintillate and to captivate. Jealousy at her success comes at a later stage in their relationship.

In return for the veranda idea, and the slip of wistaria, my host took me to an outbuilding in which was a small garden tractor. A petrol-motor drove a ribbed drum, which in turn propelled the machine. The operator walked behind, giving guidance with two handles like those of a horse-plough. There was at the back a tool-bar on which varied implements could be fitted for various jobs. My host said that the little tractor would do a gardener's daily stint in a couple of hours—ploughing, cultivating, hoeing, ridging, and moving—but that in his opinion the operator also put a day's work into two hours. Perhaps, he admitted, he had been used to too many servants in India. Certainly he had a gammy leg. Anyway, the thing had too hard a mouth for him, and if I wanted to borrow it to churn up my meadow I might.

Thus The Machine first came to Shallows.

The morning I fetched it Bert came to stand and look at it. "Whatever be 'ee for?" he inquired. "'Tisn't man enough surely for to work all out along up here."

He walked round it, and felt it, hissing to himself, like the groom he still was at heart.

"Well, I dunno, I'm sure!" he exclaimed at last. "Praaper new-fangled li'l toy it be, but 'ee won't beat old shovel for shifting muck."

I was not sure how best to employ our new ally. I affixed the cultivators, and within the hour had scarified a couple of inches of tilth over the higher half of the meadow. Bert acknowledged that this was quite a feat, and I took a rest while he gave his shovel its head, barrowing the loose soil down to the lower end. This went on all day; I scarified, and Bert shifted the soil.

By nightfall I agreed with the owner of The Machine that it was a demanding servant. It balanced but precariously on its ribbed drum, so that I had constantly to counter its efforts to lie down on one side or the other; and at the end of each straight run I had almost to lift it round. My hands were skinned at the end of the day, and my arms continued to tremble long after they had let go of the vibrating handles. True, we had shifted quite a lot of earth, but in relation to what remained it was but a surface-scratching.

I had hoped that Bert, fired by my example, would take turn and turn about with me on the second day. At first he stated flatly that he did not understand all they mechanical contrivances: not that all they sorts of puzzlers weren't right enough for they chaps as could use them, but horses was for his money. Then he put a foot up on The Machine, leant his elbow on his knee, and told of the grand houses where he had been groom among many; barrels of estate-brewed beer in the saddle-rooms; young maids in the kitchens; and two suits of livery made in London every year, to measure.

At last he said suddenly, "Start 'un up, then, and be damned to 'un!"

I explained about clutch and throttle, and tugged the starting cord. Instantly Bert let in the clutch at full revolutions and moved off at a half-trot. He spoke as he went those exclamations, half cajoling, half threatening, with which an equestrian exhorts a sidling mount. I saw at once that he was not the master. The Machine took him purposefully across the churned-up ground, heading directly for one of the great rhododendron clumps. Bert followed, trained as he had been from infancy to retain a grip on the bridles or halters of recalcitrant horses. Ponderously the pair of them ploughed into the shrubs. There was a snapping and whipping of branches, then quiet when the motor stalled. Presently Bert pushed himself backward into the open and walked towards his barrow.

"'Tisn't no manner of use me a-trying with 'ee," he said, and added with satisfaction. "I could of told'ee that as soon as I set eyes on un."

A day of two later, in despair at the slow movement of the soil to make our levels, I was wondering whether to hire a bulldozer for a morning. I was balancing mentally the time we would have to spend clearing up its mess against the time we would save on the job itself. Historical legend tells us that many scientific pioneers were inspired to their greatest discoveries by a sudden prompting which showed in a flash the clear way through a maze of wondering. Archimedes cried "Eureka" in his bathtub when he noticed his displacement. Newton was jolted into gravitation by a wind-plucked apple. Stevenson foresaw steam power as he watched the lid of a boiling kettle bob up and down.

That day, looking at The Machine, and thinking of bulldozers, I instantly saw the answer to our problem. I would make The Machine bulldoze. Within a few minutes I had affixed a stout board to The Machine's front. I chugged up to the farthest limit of the high ground and pushed a boardful of tilth to the lower end. In no time all the loose soil was shoved downhill. I removed the board, loosened up another three or four inches depth with the cultivators, and shoved again.

"'Tis wonderful to see!" exclaimed Bert.

Indeed, the board and The Machine did do a wonderful bit of work, for the edge of the plank smoothed the ground as a wood-plane cleans rough timber. There were no humps or hollows or spade-marks, and the weight of the contraption consolidated the loose earth of the built-up end.

We had a long argument about the open ditch. Bert did not want it covered up. I wanted to lay pipes, then bury it under my sweep of soil. Tessa, surprisingly, was non-committal. She agreed with neither of us, though Bert and I could think of no third alternative.

At the far end of the bed of the new lawn-to-be a low stone wall ran across the gap between the two big rhododendron clumps. It acted like the riser of a step, retaining the rough grass which stretched away at a higher level to the studio. Tessa spent an hour prowling above the little wall. Presently she called to Bert to dig at a spot she had marked with her heel. Bert went off with his shovel, giving me his usual backward glance when suspicious of the efficacy of Tessa's ideas. I took care not to catch his eye, and covertly watched him turn up a few half-hearted spadefuls to humour the Madam. All at once he began to dig with purpose and vigour, and sure enough he had tapped the spring which fed the ditch by subterranean routes.

I had once known a dowser, and had watched him pace slowly with his twitching hazel twig. I had thought to myself that his method was simpler than that of the geo-physicists. I now had to admit, however, that Tessa's way was simpler than the dowser's, requiring no twig nor intent expression of visage.

We tapped the spring into land-drains, which we now happily buried in the old ditch, but the water, now that it was denied self-expression over all the top side of the garden, flowed more thickly, and with more purpose. It spurted out of the pipes where they debouched at the edge of the drive. The former trickle had been absorbed by seepage into the ground. Now we found that the driveway was being eroded.

Bert said with deep satisfaction that us must tackle the front entrance, and make 'un respectable, like was proper in a gentleman's residence. The next thing I knew was that the drive was being widened to accommodate a ditch to drain off the water from Tessa's spring.

Thus, because we had decided to resow the meadow, half the garden became involved in the simple action. We were shown a parable of life: how one man's movement in this dense world must

E

jostle a half-dozen neighbours. We know, too, what happens when one atom is tipped off its orbit to collide with another, and this chain reaction was exemplified by the lawn.

While these subsidiary tasks were going on—the hedging to give access to the perimeter dyke; the dyke to safeguard the former laurel patch; the turfing of the laurel patch to accept the young fruit-trees; the tapping of the spring; and the ditching of the drive to take the effluence of the pipes from the spring—Tessa weeded. By hand she weeded every root of the ground elder and couch-grass out of the bare earth of the meadow. The industry of Penelope at her tapestry was but pale persistence in comparison with this. There is indeed no mechanical substitute for the final touch of the human hand.

We sowed the lawn one evening, and I hoped that all was done. But I had not taken the birds into account. I suppose that that predecessor of ours who had named the house Little Kinglet had encouraged their familiar behaviour. In summer, when all the house doors were open, blue-tits, robins, chaffinches, and even black-birds would fly into the house to perch on the furniture, or the tie-beams of the sitting-room roof; or would loop and roll in pairs right through the building. The blackbirds were so tame that they followed the progress of a garden fork closely enough to risk impalement. I believe they thought our digging was a bit of worm-hunting on their behalf. Louise claimed to know the personal habits of several individual birds, and to recognize their particular calls. It is true that quite often we would come upon her with a bird in her hand.

The morning after the sowing she came to ask me for a handful of grass seed. With the automatic parental reaction I demanded what for. It seemed that the birds had finished off all the exposed seed on the lawn, and were hard put to it to complete their breakfast. I ran out with a celerity which gratified the child.

They were all there: the two pigeons from the top of the wood; the pair of robins in whose sector of the garden the lawn lay; a host of sparrows, blue-tits, and starlings; some water-wagtails with their posterior tic; a dozen or so blackbirds, sleek as profiteers in dinner-suits; some thrushes in horsy spotted waistcoats; and presiding over all, a benign buzzard-hawk, a-perch on Bert's newly cut and laid hazel hedge. The feasters were obviously Shallows' birds, for they took no notice of me at all. They remembered, I suppose, that their ancestors had become feathered friends with the conni-vance of the bird-watcher in the days of Little Kinglet; and our children had certainly guarded the privilege.

I could not make footprints on the sown earth, so painfully levelled and smoothed. Shouts and gesticulations were ineffective. In the end I dispersed the happy horde as far as the nearest shrubs by hurling among them handfuls of gravel, like grapeshot. Even then they shaped up truculently to near misses, and nothing but a direct hit drove them up to a branch for a minute or two. For a couple of days Tessa and I flung gravel on to the lawn until it looked like the Gobi desert, and the drive was denuded.

We could obviously not continue to keep perpetual watch until the seed sprouted, neglecting all else, but the children refused to take over from us. Not even bribery would persuade them to take part in so ill-mannered a display. Savagery, however, does not lie deeply under the human skin. On the third day I made two cata-pults. Both children handled them at once with the instinctive know-how of the young. Thereafter our problem was solved, for they would stand for hours on end at the kitchen window, a tin of pebbles on the sill, shooting at every sign of movement without.

The novelty of catapulting soon wore off, and with satiety came shame at their treatment of the birds, none of whom had received more than a momentary fright. But the lawn was saved at the expense of a brief revival of the old Adam in our young.

CHAPTER FIVE

Herbaceous borders—Westhill drains—Tales of India: a maharaja showman; the merchant and the melon; a pig-chase—Drinking water—The drive

W E humans are restless animals, seeking always to improve our surroundings during the intervals between our destruction of them. Yet that which arises, Phœnix-like, from the ashes of the old is often an advance. We progress slowly: five steps forward, four steps backward. Thus painfully our species slithered out of the ooze; crept out of the jungle; set an uncertain foot on the stairway to the stars. What we do as a species on the grandest scale of which we are yet capable, we do also in humbler vein as individuals.

At Shallows, rightly or wrongly, we wanted to polish the rough natural diamond of our garden. Spring gave us a dazzling fiesta of colour, but we wanted a little brilliance during the other three seasons to point those perennial evergreens which denied winter.

During the struggles on the lawn, Tessa had been spreading wood ash in an arc about the feet of the two vast rhododendron clumps which stood at its farther edge. She had even followed ponies up and down the lane in the hope of stronger fertilizer. She now demanded that I trim back the straggling outer branches of the clumps and dig a crescent of bed round them. She maintained that a herbaceous border just here would set off the new lawn, and that its blooms would stand out splendidly against the dark green rhododendron leaves.

Bert, of course, was pleased, though he tried to make us carve geometrical beds in the sprouting lawn itself.

"'Twould look a praaper residence then," he said. He repeated instances of the acres of flower-beds he had known in the days of his glory: beds sacred to the head gardener, their blooms forbidden to the scissors of the mistress herself.

To encourage him we promised treacherously that we would sketch a few symmetrical designs while he got on with the herbaceous border. Bert tore into the work two spits deep, and we were quickly faced with two areas of untenanted earth, each about twenty yards by three.

We banished Bert to the wood while we thought above the next move. We could, I suppose, have bought a comprehensive list of plants from a nurseyman, and have had them supplied with a numbered key for correct planting in relation to size, colour, and time of flowering. But that would have been a soulless proceeding, and vastly expensive.

Furthermore, we had already discovered that nursery plants would not do at Shallows. Several times we had been beguiled by the gorgeously coloured blooms of catalogues, with such descriptions as: "Hardy perennial of tall habit. Profuse clusters of crimson flowers." With us, few of them would either grow or flower. Yet if we were surreptitiously to nip a cutting from a strange garden while our hosts were pointing out where the daffodils had given a remarkable display last month, and where the delphiniums would be a riot next month, then that cutting would survive a couple of days forgetfulness in a pocket and would later spread like a weed.

We could never account for this characteristic, but 'treat 'em rough' seemed the motto for success.

Meanwhile, we began to remember suitable plants which we already had in the garden in unsuitable places. There were lupins. They grew as if bird-sown, for certainly they would never have been set deliberately where they were. Most of these strays were alone. They struggled among heather banks; scratched for food in rockeries; wallowed in bogs; clung to rock crevices; and, bearing out the bird theory, sprouted from old stumps and the forks of trees.

Except for the quaintness of their habitat, these varied plants gave little to the eye, for the power of the common species is in their quantity. A dozen roots scattered over an acre are lost. A dozen grouped have the strength of unity, and claim attention.

We collected what we could, and the numbers went some way

towards filling one border. As to the other border, we decided to beg from neighbours, and to augment the floral alms with splits and layerings.

Meanwhile we debated whether to follow an Eastern idea of which Tessa had heard: to arrange that the bed was occupied each month by one solitary magnificent specimen of whatever genus was then in flower. The principle was that of the Chinese who places but a single champion bloom in a vase. Our trouble, we knew, would be to cultivate such prizewinners month by month, and if we succeeded, to keep them from the children, especially Johanna, who was an indefatigable gatherer. Wherever we went out of doors we found her offerings to the small people of the woods and rocks. Flowers were laid out on flat stones; at the mysterious clefts in the trunks of our witches' oaks; at the gravelled sides of the quiet pools. Were we to rear a really magnificent flower within child-reach we knew that it would be given to Oberon himself.

We had just come to a decision that we must beg roots and cuttings, and were standing on the young lawn before the gaping earth of the empty bed, when old Robertson came up the drive. Behind him were two men from one of the local builders.

A year of post-war Britain had aged old Robertson by a decade. Now he looked close on his seventy years. He gave his usual rhetorical greeting of "How goes the battle?" I returned the query, expecting an answer, and interested to hear what it could be, for old Robertson was a frequent refugee to Shallows at morning coffee time. Thus I knew that recently he had torn a finger on his circular-saw, which was driven by the successor of that primitive mammoth which I had once cranked for him; that the part of his drive near the lane had been washed away by one of our streams; that the Westhill thatch was full of leaks; and that two of his wife's sows, which she had bought to augment his pension, had not stood to the boar, their bulk being due not to incipient motherhood but to gross overeating at the expense of Robertson's pension.

I did not think, remembering some other adversities as well, that much else remained to befall old Robertson. However, he said that now the water had dried up. It was the one thing that had never given him a moment's worry, he said, since that first day when

Tessa and I had started his old engine for him and had waited while he tried the electric pump. He spoke as if this last stroke were sharper than a serpent's tooth.

I do not think that Tessa and I are unkind people, but the Shallows water has never given trouble, and we could not help but listen to old Robertson with smug sympathy. After all, he had a house, not a growth, which is all that Shallows was.

It appeared that there was another difficulty, besides the water. The telephone was dead again, and might Jim the Plumber use ours to ring up his boss and ask advice?

Jim the Plumber was gone for some time. When he came back he said:

"'Tis surely a praaper old puzzle. The boss's father done summat with all these old drains when Log 'Ut were built. It did all belong along of Westhill once, see. But boss can't remember rightly where water did all come from, though his dad told him once before he was took mortal bad."

Tessa and I knew of one cistern which had nothing to do with old Robertson's problem, and that was the brick chamber whose cast-iron man-hole was stamped "Westhill Water Supply." We did not mention this.

"Boss says as he thinks he do remember 'twas said cistern for Westhill was in Log 'Ut meadow. Us'll look round. If us can find cistern 'twill be simple for to follow up pipes and dig'un out. Though 'twill be a big job, mind," Jim the Plumber added with threatening satisfaction.

Hitherto the whole affair had been old Robertson's burden, and we had been content to give sympathy and advice. But now, with shocking suddenness, we were involved. There was, I recalled, some clause in our deeds which adjured us to allow occupiers of Westhill to search out their water. This, I thought, was the million to one chance against which some lawyer had guarded. His mischievous ghost was come over a half-century to plague us. The lawn, so palely green and new, would be turned into a piece of arable land. Probably my levelling operations had damaged the Westhill pipes, just as my pickaxe had destroyed others some time back. Old Robertson would be likely to sue me. My persistent

destruction of his easements and amenities might take me, not to
the civil court, but the criminal.

Jim the Plumber's mate, a long, thin lad, with a long, thin face
like a ferret, had been nosing round while we talked, and now cried
that he'd found 'un. He was scrabbling at a man-hole in the middle
of the lawn, close to the levelled bit for the badminton court. I
knew all about this particular cistern, or, at any rate, all that it was
necessary to know. It was choked with water-weed, and the only
outlet which I had ever been able to find bore away from Westhill.
The purpose of its construction was as obscure as that of the stone
avenues which had been laid by the ancient small dark men on the
moor above. I hastened to assure every one that 'twouldn't be no
manner of good a-digging of 'un up.

Old Robertson, used to his seventy-eight servants and the
golden orb, was for strolling off while the white man's burden was
borne by Jim the Plumber. But I could not tear myself away.

It was a long battle, but I remained firm against the digging.
Finally Jim the Plumber said that he would return whence he had
come to fetch some dye. We could then see just where the outlet
from the cistern led, for it had, surely, to follow the dip of the ground
to the stream beyond the house.

"'Lessn 'un goes t'Westhill," said the thin lad, whom I disliked.
Jim the Plumber rattled off in an antique van, while old Robertson
came round to the veranda to have his usual coffee. Bert strolled by
at the crucial moment, as was his custom, and, with his usual surprised gratitude, accepted a cup, saying a fellow could fare worse if
there weren't no beer about. He and old Robertson swapped tales
about India, in which country Bert had once served the British Raj
as an insubordinate horse-gunner.

Bert's tales were always horrific: about the times when they had
galloped the limbers through the mobs of rioting Indians; or how
a draft of green troops, new to the heat of the country, had been
kept too long on parade, and had fallen in neat swathes, cut down
by heat-stroke; or how the wine of the country, represented by
distillates little known to the western world, destroyed the optic
nerve at a gulp.

Old Robertson was more subtle. One of his most pleasing

anecdotes was of a visit to a certain Maharajah who was a renowned sadist. The prince had arranged a circus, which was opened by introducing a panther and a jackass simultaneously into the ring. To the Maharajah's annoyance, the panther lay down against the palisade on the shady side, while the jackass grazed quietly in the middle. Attendants gave the panther the equivalent of the bird by prodding him with long poles, whereupon the beast arose and strolled over to the opposite fence. Unfortunately he passed close behind the ass, who, without lifting his head from the grass, let fly with both hind legs, hammering such a tattoo on the panther's ribs that no further pole-prodding could persuade him to move. We were to hear the climax of this ruler's career as showman. It appeared that he possessed a waning mistress who had once been a tight-rope walker, and whom, when he had tired of her, he persuaded to give a display of the art which she had discarded. When she was in mid-transit, the prince, carrying playfulness to the point of horseplay, had a gentleman of his household cut the guys which strained the poles between which the rope was strung. This was the end of the act, and of the mistress. It was also the end of the prince, for the British Raj, in the skilful way which formerly was natural to it, dismissed the prince from his authority. Very many of old Robertson's stories illustrated how erring rulers were measured against Britain's standards of behaviour, and if they fell far short were discarded.

His motto might have been: "We came, we taught, we abdicated."

Old Robertson and his kind served a principle, rather than carved a career. My neighbour was, I knew, quite an impoverished man, despite the opportunities which he must have had for reward. He unconsciously gave evidence of one of these opportunities, and of his reaction to it, when we were discussing the corruption which is so rife in the East that it is the normal, rather than the abnormal.

As prime minister of a native state old Robertson was petitioned constantly to intercede; to further an attempt to gain a favour; to give access to justice to those who could not buy it. Once an important merchant asked old Robertson to obtain a favour for him from the ruler. He offered nothing but a single melon as a friendly

gift. He must have mistaken the reason for some hesitation which
Robertson had shown in pursuing the request, for he beseeched him
then and there to open the melon. At his insistence Robertson
sliced it open, and found the inside to be stuffed with gems.

I asked what he did then.

"I told him that this was a fruit which I was forbidden to eat,"
said old Robertson.

Bert snorted.

"None of they Indians never offered me no rubies!" he exclaimed. "Else I wouldn't be working for a living no more."

Noblesse oblige is indeed a mortification.

To console Bert, however, old Robertson told the story of his
one lapse from incorruptibility. It appeared that he visited the
districts of his state, bearing justice in his person. At one place the
usual long list of hearings awaited him. When he was about to reach
the last case, however, he was distracted by cries of "Pig! Pig!"
The headman left his side for a moment, and returned to say that
report told of a fine boar, an emperor of pigs, which was playing
havoc in the fields near by. He had already sent for the sahib's
horse and spear.

Old Robertson relived the chase as he sat on the veranda in our
peaceful stillness, broken only by the ripple of water and his own
quiet voice. Then he told how later on he became friends with the
headman, and on his visits the two of them used to talk much of
philosophy and the way of life. Once they discussed the corruption which was but a question of price; that, as they said in the West,
every man had his price. Old Robertson denied that. He said that
in the West there were many men who could not be bribed. He
said that he himself would never take a bribe.

The headman gazed for a while into the middle air, seeing a
picture there. Without moving his eyes he asked whether old
Robertson remembered that day some years before when a cry of
"Pig" had interrupted his judicial hearings; and what fine sport it
had shown him.

Old Robertson indeed remembered.

The headman wondered if old Robertson recalled the last hearing
on his list that morning; perhaps, after all, he could not recall it.

He had been lured from it by the boar, and had forgotten to sit upon it before he left the district with the dawn next day. Perhaps, the headman thought, it was in order to say, after this long lapse of time, that the elders of the village had not thought it in the best interest of justice that this case should be heard just then. There had been long discussion about what gift might best persuade old Robertson to miss it; some suggested a jewel; some a horse; others, without finesse, money.

It was the headman himself, versed in the ways of the British, who had advised the boar.

"But, Sahib," he said, "I did not advise it on grounds of economy, for to arrange for a wild boar to appear in those fields at that exact moment cost us more than the price of a charger."

Shallows had always a Shangri-La atmosphere; a timelessness which provoked reminiscence as much as futuristic speculation. As with old Robertson, the ageless thoughts might be personal; as with other people, they might flit from deductions about the origins of terrestrial life drawn from the clues imprisoned in the rocks, to astral navigation, where creeping movement is measured in light years.

So timeless, indeed, was that particular morning, that we had all forgotten Jim the Plumber, until he walked round the house to say, unnecessarily, that here he were ag'in. The boss had cast his mind back to the time his father had given him his little talk on Westhill water, and, though it was close on fifty years before, thought he remembered something about a cistern in Westhill's own garden. Meanwhile Jim, having fetched the dye, had felt he ought to use it, and had put a large quantity into the cistern in Shallows' new lawn. We all got up, and spent an exciting half-hour moving rapidly from mouth to mouth of the many pipes which drained into the nearer stream.

"Reckon us'll never know where they pipes run from that old cistern," said Jim the Plumber at last. "Us'll off dig around in Westhill."

Old Robertson became as apprehensive as I had recently been, and accompanied Jim and the thin-faced lad to put some restraint on their excavations.

The children had been playing within distant earshot in a woody grotto which had only just been made accessible. It was an attractive miniature ravine which ran from the drive to the fish-pond. It was neatly arched by some splendid hollies, but had been so boggy that none of us had set foot inside until I dug a water-way along its bottom. This had at once shown a much greater volume than seepage would have given, and leapt into full flow at the top end beside the drive. I had assumed that I had tapped yet another of the Shallows springs, the more so since the sides of the grotto had dried out once the water was contained in a course.

That morning the children surpassed themselves in vocal effect soon after old Robertson and Jim had left. I was sure that mud or damp was the cause of the delight, and went over to see before Tessa could blame me for making the place fit to enter, but not fit to play in. But the excitement was not because of mud or mayhem. It was because the water-course was flowing bright blue.

Jim the Plumber at last uncovered a cistern in a bamboo thicket within Westhill garden. The inflow was gushing merrily. Its pipe clearly ran under the lane to some undiscovered source at Shallows. The outflow to Westhill, however, was blocked by infiltrating roots, weed, and frogs. This occasioned no revulsion in old Robertson, used as he was to equally primitive systems in India. Nor would it have worried any other local folk, one and all of whom had their little periodic troubles with water supplies. Indeed, the ups and downs of water-tables, and the ins and outs of foreign matter and bodies in relation to pipes, were almost as fertile sources of conversation as were the ailments of lighting plants.

I wonder if we all fuss too much about cleanliness. There is that old saying that we will eat a peck of dirt before we die. Perhaps we *ought* to eat or drink the peck in order to give our resistance germs an enemy to exercise themselves upon. Medical inoculation achieves just that. Possibly the "untouched by hand from factory to consumer," the "triple-filtered and chlorinated," demand is overdone. More than once I have been in mountain country with companions who hesitated to drink from the mountain springs whose fountains were filtered by the body of mother earth. They deserved the fate of Tantalus.

Yet these same abstainers from a natural purity which has not been stamped with the seal of the Water Board, will drink their beer with the more greed when at last they descend to an inn. They drink it out of tankards which have been cleansed in the traditional manner of the British inn, by a quick dip under the bar into a chipped enamel bowl of brown liquid, just warm enough to animate bacilli.

At any rate, if people do not get their intake of germs in one way they do in another.

Bert Westmacott was a proud man when the green lawn overlay the roughness of the former meadow, and the two borders lay crescent-shaped about the foot of the rhododendron banks. True, the beds were very bare at first, but the principle was established.

Bert now began to worry about the drive. For the standard of our establishment the drive was quite an area. There were about forty yards of it from the gate to the house, where it widened into a sweep where a car might turn with just one reverse. Then it ran on to the garage, thirty yards away, up by the top linhay. The whole lot took three days to hoe, and in summer needed hoeing monthly. Bert was quite happy about this, feeling that a man at work with a hoe was a part of a gentleman's drive. At current wage-rates, Tessa and I were not at all happy that our drive should be lent an air of gentility by a permanent Bert.

We were fortunate in having a supply of gravel from the two streams, and after we had cleaned up the surfaces of the drive and paths we spread the fine pebbles. The origin of this gravel was a mystery. There was no source for it on our property, nor, as we found when we tried to trace its home, on the moor above. For all their length, the streams ran through peat, their beds studded by granite boulders. Yet our gravel was not eroded granite, but was of little smooth pebbles the colour of sand. The gravel settled in small banks at the edge of pools where a swirl of water washed it. Although we carried it away in quantity, lifting all we could find, the very next flood would build the banks anew.

When the first dressing was on the drive the place certainly looked very smart. But in our little pocket of the moor all green things grew. Shrubs, trees, flowers, vegetables, and weeds grew and grew all together in a fine comradeship of life. *Tropæolum speciosum*, scarlet-flowered, berried in electric blue, raced the white convolvulus to the top of the rhododendron banks; honeysuckle swarmed over trees and porches, and climbed up itself when there was no other support; azaleas and rhododendrons rooted themselves in the very lichen of the rocks; ferns flourished high in the forks of the oaks. We could not expect our gravelled drive to remain barren in so fructifying an air. Nor did it. Within the month it was green with dandelion, chickweed, thistle, and moss.

It was all very well for Bert to hoe again, but when he shovelled his heaps of weed into a barrow he shovelled the gravel with them, and back we had to go to the stream to replenish it. I foresaw the maintenance as an endless chain; a putting on of gravel, and a taking away of gravel with weed added. Fearful of this Sisyphusian future, I at last experimented with sodium chlorate, mixing the crystals in a big water-butt, and sprinkling the drive with a watering-can.

Bert came on me not forewarned, and watched with puzzlement. He inquired whatever for were I encouraging they old weeds, with the drive damp after rain, anyways, m' dear. I explained about the sodium, and that it went farther and was more effective in the damp. He was not so much sceptical as displeased that he might, perhaps, never again grace our entrance with a hoe as the staff of office, and I had to put him in good humour by offering a slice of jungle to slash. For three or four days the young weeds seemed to flourish as so many infant green bay-trees; then they browned, and died. It was a full six months before new seedlings thrust through the gravel. Now we have a half-yearly routine of sodium sprinkling. The drive and paths stay clean; the hoe is laid to rest as far as they are concerned; but Bert has a wistful look whenever he admires the gravel.

CHAPTER SIX

*Local gentry—The cost of living in the country—Country people
—The girl from Essen*

WHEN we came to Shallows it was ten years since either Tessa or I had lived in the country, and most of that decade had been filled by war, together with its approach and aftermath. Now we found that there was much change, although in that large area served by Rattleford most of the change was superficial. The rearguard of the old order who were housed round about had jettisoned no essentials in their retreat from economic enemies.

There were around Rattleford ex-sailors, soldiers, airmen, Anglo-Indians, authors, artists, ex-Secret-Intelligence-Service agents, and even ne'er-do-wells. These local gentry—as Bert did not scruple to call them—had that rustic *savour faire* which is one of the obligatory qualifications for that class. They knew a little about several rural subjects; about flowers, fruit, vegetables, forestry, fish, game, natural history, ornithology, agriculture, stock, geology, and even meteorology. Most of them, in addition to this general knowledge, were expert in at least one branch of country lore.

A large proportion of our neighbours had moved to the district since the War. In some way the influx had snowballed. Each newcomer, it seemed to me, must have told two friends of the excellence of the district; and each of the two friends, having sampled this desirability, must have told two more. Anyway, there they were, men of war and men of Empire, jobless now that war was done and the Empire a shrinking Commonwealth.

A common factor to most of these newcomers was ignorance of post-war economic conditions, for many of them had come straight from overseas. They came equipped with pensions added to private means of a sort, and set themselves up in the style to which they would have expected to become accustomed in retirement.

Tessa and I, who aspired to no style at all, watched many a newcomer run through an identical gamut of housekeeping.

There would be a large car, and a small one for the wife's shopping. There would be a servant or two in the house; a gardener without; and sometimes a groom. Within twelve months a particular family would look bewildered, rather than worried. When we met them we would feel that no casual talk claimed their inner attention, but that their brains were clicking over like adding-machines. Then we would one day come upon them in cheerful, boisterous mood.

"We've got rid of the big car," they would say, ordering us a drink of an expensive nature. "It was a liability in these lanes. We've always used the little one, anyway, ever since we've been here."

Then, casually, a few minutes later:

"Know anything about mushrooms? Thought we might try some in the garage now the Daimler's gone. Don't suppose there's any money in it, but it'd be a bit of a hobby, you know."

Then after a pause:

"There *isn't* any money in it, I suppose?"

And the wistful accent would creep in.

Within six months the adding-machines would be clicking again, and Tessa and I would be content with the superficialities of conversation until the joyous day when we would hear that the gardener had gone.

"I've always been an active man, you know. If we hadn't handed over India I wouldn't have been retired for donkey's years. Got to keep myself occupied. Always been interested in gardening. In fact, both of us have. We've got a really good kitchen garden, but that fellow we had didn't know a radish from a broccoli. We're going to tackle it ourselves."

We would wait for the addendum:

"What do you think of cloches? They claim they do bring stuff on early. Do you know, we wondered if there mightn't be quite a market round here for garden produce."

The mushrooms and market-garden would prove to be more expensive in upkeep than the car and man which they had replaced, and there would be a black season of blighted bonhomie until the announcement that those two useless women in the kitchen had gone.

"Spent all my time stamping cards for 'em and carting them backward and forward on their days off. Anyway, my wife likes cooking. Of course, she never got the chance in India. She's looking forward no end to trying her hand."

In the finish, most of our neighbours were forced to temper their establishments to the economic storm. Like old Robertson's, the daily greeting was "How's the battle?" With Napoleon, one and all might have said, "Ask of me anything but Time." For leisure was gone in a countryside where depreciated currency would no longer buy help.

Rural life costs more than urban: that is why there is a drift from the deep countryside to the cities. There are few country parishes which do not have a long list of houses to sell or to let, in spite of a national shortage of dwellings. Only in those dormitory areas within reach of, and with good communications to, cities is there a strong demand.

The cost of rural living is interrelated with lack of rural amenities. For instance, many districts are without mains electricity. A private generating set is an inefficient substitute whose maintenance is far more costly than would be light and power from the grid.

Again, the countryman pays dearly for the unsophisticated charm of the bootlace and liquorice village shop. Gossip is to be had there; and a customer's special preferences in shag, mints, calico, and scythe handles are reached from the shelves or hooks before he has to ask for them. But these intimate services are paid for by an extra penny or two added to most purchases. The village shop-keeper is not much constrained by competition. He knows that there is not much choice within the village, and that a disgruntled customer must conceal his dissatisfaction, or else spend money on petrol or fares to travel to the nearest town. The village surcharge is a form of blackmail concealed by quaintness and hallowed by custom. All the same, the dowdy village shop is a collective institu-tion which I would not like to see displaced by the white porcelain and chromium of the chain-shore, for all that gaudy Jezebel's

F

professional efficiency and cut rates. The welcome of the village shop is fairly genuine. The smile of the chain-store is as mirthless as that of a toothpaste advertisement; the affection is for the wallet, not the customer.

In Rattleford the tradesmen had us all firmly hooked, and knew it. When a captive became restive he was treated to an under-the-counter course for a week or two. A sly Devonian shopkeeper would slip him a packet of milk chocolate, rather than plain; proper cigarettes in place of some fly-by-night brand; a pound of pork sausages with the weekly meat. The customer preened himself, and was put on his honour to remain within his unbarred prison.

It was Bert Westmacott's wife who confirmed an opinion on country housekeeping which Tessa had been urging on me. Bert Westmacott's wife, like Bert himself, had served in great houses, and had climbed in the end to the position of housekeeper. She knew what was what, and they were indeed fortunate summer visitors who stayed with her. I happened to be by one day when some of her guests were leaving to return to their own crude cookery and service, and heard them deliver a valedictory address in praise, particularly, of the food they had received. They spoilt the declamation, however, by adding that food was, of course, so much easier to come by in the country: home-reared ham and bacon; fowls; eggs; rabbits; vegetables.

Mrs Bert put them right, donning that expression of admonitory propriety which is at its most effective in the upper servant.

She began by pointing out that the field which they rented for their pigs and chickens was uphill at some distance from the cottage. Bert being at work all day, it fell to her to do most of the care-taking. As far as the pig was concerned—the one whose remains had inspired their veneration—twice a day through the rain and snow of the previous winter she had carried his buckets of food to him. The meal ration, she pointed out, was notoriously insufficient, and much of Bert's leisure had been employed in scouring the countryside for supplementary diet. Mrs Westmacott cautiously gave no details of these murky expeditions of Bert—some of which I had shared, since a car with an extra large, lockable boot was essential equipment. She did, though, mention the difficulties of boiling daily a cauldron of potatoes over the primitive wash-house fire.

All in all, if their labour was counted in at the very lowest rates, the bacon and hams in the kitchen were worth as much as the most expensive off-ration meats. A man on agricultural wage-rates could not afford these, and must therefore grow his own pig and add his own labour. Many town and industrial workers could afford to buy off-ration delights, using their extra pay, in effect, to purchase exemption from any work in connexion with their rearing.

So it was, too, with the fowls and eggs. There were times, said Mrs Westmacott, when a mouthful of egg would choke her by evoking memories of the bitter winter days spent paddling about Bert's damp field. Bitter, too, were the memories conjured up by a nice roast carcase. Day-old chicks, she said, were costly, and the hovers and brooders and arks even more costly. It was heart-breaking to put dear food into the chicks for half a year so that they might feed a fox when they were on the point of lay.

The visitors began to look as uncomfortable as did that mythical guest who, after a splendid repast, was told by his host that the main dish had been one of the guest's own children. The rashers, fowls, and eggs, eaten so lightheartedly, were metamorphosed into another person's blood, sweat, and tears.

But, still, there were the vegetables. The visitors, sidling towards their car, mentioned the delicious flavour of produce fresh picked. Mrs Bert looked darkly at the garden. It was hard, she said, that a man had to go digging and hoeing and staking after he had already done a fair day's work. Still, there was no choice. The price was prohibitive in Rattleford, and there were no cheap markets like in the towns, where the big market-gardeners could afford to send their stuff at a fractional profit. Although, by the time the pests had had a go, and the Dartmoor bullocks and Harry George Pengelly's Scotch sheep had broken in a time or two, it might be cheaper to buy them even at Rattleford prices. The only drawback to that was carrying them back home two and a half miles up the lane.

No! Mrs Bert summed up. The towns were the places for cheap housekeeping, with off-ration foods in the shops which never appeared in the country, and wage-rates which gave people a chance to buy them.

The urban visitors drove soberly away. Like so many, I expect they themselves came only to the country to play, knowing and caring little of those who lived in the country to work.

Townspeople use the countryside as an amenity, as a super-colossal park. Their own urban lives do not school them to understand that all their grand offices, their smart sophistication, their places of entertainment—in fact, both their livelihood and recreation—are located in the half of a social pyramid whose broad and stable base in all countries is filled by the peasant and the land he tills.

Rusticity is, of course, as much a calling as are the professions of healing and the Church. If it were not an urge which overrides calculation few of us would be rustics.

Tessa and I wondered often why we were so in love with our shambling house, and with its wild surround of rock and rushing streams, pointed so incongruously with the tropical colours of our shrubs and many of our plants. But a man falls in love with a particular woman, and they say that the reverse is true, too, even though by and large all humans are much the same. They have eyes, ears, a nose, a mouth, arms and legs. They are poor swimmers, awkward walkers, uncertain climbers, and cannot fly at all without mechanical contrivance. Yet in their pairs they step into a dazed love-dance, each with a picked partner out of the same mass-production mould. It must, therefore, be the unseen ego which binds each to each.

So it was with Shallows. We were in love with the spirit of the place.

In this past decade of social reorientation the countryside materially has changed more than the town, but, paradoxically, it has altered less in spirit. Up to the recent War a touch of the feudal system had persisted in the country. The squire and the parson had excercised a leadership derived from their respective offices. Each in his sphere, temporal and spiritual, had wielded the strong influence of benevolent autocrats. That influence is gone. The old squire is dead. His son, perhaps, died too in aeroplane or ship or stricken tank. If he survived physically, he certainly could not continue to survive financially on the contracted acres of his inheritance. He has moved in most cases to the places of business. The big house is sold to a rootless stranger who has succeeded in that business world, or to an institution, or it has fallen derelict.

If the country folk may no longer look to their squire for practical advice and leadership, neither do they often look to the parson for spiritual guidance. Economic conditions have driven away the squirearchy. Wider education and a broader mental outlook among the parishioners have reduced in their eyes the stature of the parson.

To a great extent the parish has lost its identity now that its problems are not discussed among and solved by the chief figures within its community. Self-government of its own small affairs is nearly lost. The County Councils, town-based and urban in their approach, run the rural areas, and in turn they themselves are now largely run by the metropolitan minds of Westminster and White-hall. The graded devolution of control from Parliament has now gathered into its fingers more strings than it can adroitly handle. Those far-off parish puppets with a low density of voters to the square mile, traditionally unvocal, suffer the worst inattention.

Despite the loss of much which held country life together, some qualities remain from the old days. The most endearing is that class-conscious classlessness of the countryman. All instinctively have that essence of social awareness which is translated into English in the phrase 'knowing one's place,' and in the result no one is gauche in any company, since all are sure of where they stand. A swineherd on a duke's estate is much easier in the presence of his employer than is a machinist in that of a factory superintendent. The reason is because rusticity is indeed a calling, and any two people who have embraced it meet on common ground, with mutual interests. Both are in the service of the ancient mother goddess, Earth. They observe the same rites and share in the performance of them.

The material balance is awry, but this old ease of comradeship remains.

Around Rattleford, as in most country districts, a new type of countryman is being blended into the community. He is the type formerly known by the term 'gentleman farmer,' which had a derogatory implication. It used to be held that the nouns 'gentleman' and 'farmer' were antipathetic, and so cancelled one another, turning the man thus christened into a social and agricultural drone. It is true that some of these people were once upon a time drones, and could then afford so to be. Now it is not so.

A host of young ex-servicemen with their young wives has settled upon the land. They apply regulated minds and good physique to the tasks of growing, as once they applied them to the tasks of killing. Their coming is profoundly important. They are the leavening which country ways and country blood need from time to time if methods are not to become obsolete and blood stale. They have had enough experience in human relationships to slide unobtrusively into the rural community, blending with their neighbours rather than elbowing them aside.

The majority seem to be making a success of their chosen living, but I sometimes wonder whether financial success will keep their families to the task. It is the women who will become restive.

Already there is a great exodus of retired folk, folk of private means, and folk who do not live directly off the land—authors, artists, and the like—to the all-mains-services towns. Similarly, the distaff side of the new, young recruits to agriculture may demand some of the rewards of success. They may ask for shops, theatres, cinemas, and concerts. At the least they may ask for electricity, made roads, extended public transport services. Without these amenities no young wife can long persuade domestic help to remain with her. Financial success will purchase no rewards.

The husband has progressed from wooden plough and oxen to a tractor with hydraulically controlled implements. The wife remains near enough in the Stone Age. At any rate, it is not an exaggeration to say that she often lingers in those Victorian conditions which had made her grandmother into an elderly woman at twenty-five. She puts up with them; maid-servants will not. A maid-servant is no personal luxury in a farmhouse. She is as much a farm employee as is the cowman or ploughman, for the women-folk of a farm share in much of the men's work.

The non-agricultural residents around Rattleford—the tiro

cloche gardeners and mushroom growers—were a most friendly lot.
Tessa and I had wondered what the modern country custom of
acquaintanceship was: whether people called, or whether one waited
a year for acknowledgment. We realized that we might remain
unvisited for a very long time, since Shallows was not a house to
which people could well pay a call. Often the drive was barred by
some drainage scheme which lay athwart it. Even were some dainty
lady to penetrate to the house, she would be bewildered by the multi-
plicity of doors. Card-case in hand, she would feel as uncomfortable
as a child, all keyed up for the occasion, who does not know to whom
she should present her nosegay. Quite likely, we thought, Bert
would pop round a corner and would shoo the caller away as an
unwanted canvasser.

Only one formal call was made upon us. Tessa, in an old pair of
trousers and Wellington boots full of water owing to a miscalcula-
tion in the stream where we dug the gravel, received the visitor.
The proper duration of stay of fifteen minutes was not by one
second exceeded, owing to Louise's appearance with a toad which
she set upon the window-seat of the sitting-room in order that it
might regale itself upon flies. As Louise explained, toads are fussy
and will not look at dead flies filched from spider's webs.

However, in place of personal formal visits we found that anonymous voices would speak over the telephone.

"You won't know who I am, but we're having drinks next
Friday at half-past six. Do come along if you can."

Sometimes there would be a *quid pro quo*—the quid being pun-
ningly the financial query in every one's mind.

"Henry's read your husband's book about upland farming. He
wants to ask how Welsh black cattle would do on Dartmoor."

Quite often the voice would say good-bye without disclosing
name or address, for Devonian inconsequence is very contagious.

These cocktail parties, of course, supplanted the afternoon tea
and dinner parties of pre-War times. An elegant cocktail party is
easy to stage-manage without help; a dinner party impossible.

Thus are those graces lost which bolster human status; and thus
is the atmosphere gone in which intellect might expand in leisured
conversation. You might say that the art of entertainment has gone

native, all for the lack of a serving-maid. Not that anyone turned up their noses at the Rattleford cocktail parties. At many of them a hundred guests would jam the narrow lanes, converging from the nooks and cranies which lay on the scarp of the moor. They swarmed like wasps to a jampot, or, as one local misogynist said, like buzzards to a carcase.

This lack of domestic help, itself caused largely by the lack of rural amenities, is having a great effect on country life. It is not so much that the would-be employers desire service as a luxury, but as a means to release their time for more positive purposes than the negation of household tasks.

Tessa tried for a long while to find local help. There was none. Those girls who were not employed by the hotels or tradesmen had moved away. Some one, somewhere, in authority had recognized this rural dearth, for we learned of an official plan by whose provisions continental girls were imported as domestics. Tessa returned one day from a trip to Okehampton. She wore a self-satisfied expression, and demanded a cheque for a third-class single fare to Essen. I asked the reason for this sudden whim, and, without going so far as to offer the price of a second-class ticket, suggested that I might give her enough for the return journey. It appeared, however, that the money was not for her, but was to be handed to the Okehampton Labour Exchange, who had consented to import a girl for our very own use.

As time went by expectation was dimmed to apathy, and finally extinguished in forgetfulness. It was then that I was mystified by an urgent male voice over the telephone which begged me to drive at once to Exeter to meet my girl, who was even then nearing the station in an express train. I said that I was already married, and that my informant was probably connected to the wrong number. The strange voice demanded with agitation whether I no longer wanted a girl, then. If so, I should have said so before. As it was, I would certainly have to pay her fare back to London.

I became wary of this, believing that I was the victim of an attempt to demand money with menaces. I inquired the name of the unknown caller, wondering whether he or I would be Mr 'A' in court, and was momentarily taken aback by the coolness with which he said that his name did not matter, but that he was speaking from Okehampton Labour Exchange. This, I thought, would certainly hit the headlines.

Tessa wandered through the house on her way from the herbaceous border to the stream. She asked if that was Okehampton. If so, she had meant to tell me that she had had a card from them warning us to stand by for our girl from Essen.

Tessa and I were going out that night to attend one of the innumerable Rattleford cocktail parties, and I realized that time was pressing more insistently than usual. I travelled the twenty miles to Exeter more quickly than usual in the Allard, which was known up and down the lanes as "that car of yours."

I failed to meet the train by a minute or two, and realized it when I saw in the booking office a bunch of sturdy females in white ankle socks who were clustered around an efficient Anglo-Saxon woman with a fringe and a notebook.

Among these, I thought, is my quarry. From among them I will receive the buxom and capable *Hausfrau* or *Fräulein* who will smooth our domestic path. And, indeed, each individual of the group except one looked as powerfully capable as a steamroller. This exception was sallow and bent, dressed in sombre black, like a bedraggled starling.

Even so, I felt that the law of averages was on my side until the efficient Anglo-Saxon inquired my name, flipped through her book, and called forth the sodden starling. I asked in a heartbroken whisper whether I might not have another one. Almost I offered to toss for it. But I was silenced with a remark that each was earmarked—like imported cattle, I thought—and would I sign here for mine.

Thus it was that Else and I climbed into the Allard—she without a word of our hostile tongue, and I in a hurry, and with foreboding as to the girl's future. It may be that Else was delivered a little breathless, and perhaps a little startled, at the door of Shallows where it lay under Kestor Rock, surrounded by the enigmatic skyline of Dartmoor.

Tessa, however, came out to welcome her, as did the children with their collection of toads, newts in jam-jars, kittens, and a stray foxhound. Our Else jumped out of the car, bag in hand, ran into the house, rushed into the nearest room, and slammed and locked the door. Fortunately it was the room which had been prepared for her.

We waited a while, and Tessa tried to cajole her into reappearing by the use of a species of German which she had gathered at her Swiss school. This was not sufficiently a lingua franca to be effective. In the end Bert turned up to mind the children—since I had ordered him before I knew of our help's arrival—and we left him in charge.

On our return from our cocktail party I asked Bert how he had got on with the nervous foreigner. He didn't know for sure. Her had stuck her head out of the door as he was a-drawing from the cider barrel in the back hall, and when he had said "Hallo, m' dear, you come along out o' there and have a drop," her head had shot back in again like a scary little old rabbit.

It was three days before we enticed Else from her room in day-light, though she must have unlocked herself at night, since the food which we placed outside her door was always gone by morning. In making these nocturnal offerings we felt that we were but fol-lowing moorland custom, for many a lonely farmstead to this day puts the pixies' supper outside the house ready for collection. Very sensibly they add something extra when a Princetown convict is loose. This saves trouble for every one.

In the interval between Else's brief personal appearance on arrival and her emergence from retreat seventy-two hours later we made many telephone calls. The Ministry of Labour, like U.N.O., refused at first to intervene in a domestic issue. We then appointed a one-man fact-finding commission in the person of a neighbour who spoke fluent German. The commission had difficulty at the start, and reported that the girl spoke a dialect whose relationship to German was as that of the Gorbals tongue to Oxford English. With practice, however, a tenuous communication was established through the panels of the barred door. The situation bristled with misunderstandings, for our Else had come to England expressly to join an elder sister as a ward-maid in a Midland hospital. She had, it seemed, mistaken Exeter for a Midland city, and had been dis-appointed not to be met by her sister. The disappointment was as nothing to her terror when she was abducted by a man in a maniacal hurry, and, after a ride which might have figured in the *Götter-dämmerung*, was decanted in as remote a spot as girl had ever been made away in.

At least we now knew what had prompted the locking of the door. It was when we had conducted a complicated and expensive series of three-cornered telephone talks with Else's sister and the Ministry of Labour that we enticed her forth to hear the news that she might leave for the Midlands next morning.

It was, I recall, one of our most beautiful moorland days, the air so still that the courses of the streams could be traced by ear alone, and the round white balls of cloud hanging like carnival balloons from a blue ceiling. Tessa led Else on to the veranda to join us for coffee, and, as we sat, said involuntarily to the German girl:

"Don't you think it's beautiful?"

Else hunched herself up until she looked even more like a sick starling than when first I had seen her. She glanced at the crisp distant skyline, the splendid trees, the liquid diamonds in the water, and the thousand blossoms of a hundred colours, some of which roofed the very place where she sat. She surprised us by commenting in halting English. She said:

"In my part of Essen—we have five cinemas."

We have not since tried again to find help in the house. The house and garden are indivisible, and we really cannot put applicants through a test to discover whether they like our wilderness as much as we do.

CHAPTER SEVEN

Robertson decides to leave—The sale—Garden tractors—The Machine comes to Shallows—Pan, spirit of the woods

OLD Robertson at Westhill shared the shelf on which Shallows rested, though he was not so close under the sheltering lee of the moor. He loved our small oasis as much as we did, and would, I think, have lived out his days there in great happiness. But in post-War Britain the tide was too eddying and unpredictable to allow the flotsam of a past era to lie peacefully in a backwater.

Old Robertson had moved to Westhill, I believe, in the hope that the spaciousness of the house and the charm of its surroundings would attract his sons and grandchildren to make long and frequent visits. But the restlessness of the ex-serviceman had stayed with the sons, and one by one they left the shelter of their peacetime jobs to venture anew in far countries.

Nothing was left to old Robertson except the daily chores which the pension, won by a life-time of service, could not mitigate. The decision to leave was made after the accident at the saw bench. I had been urgently called over to Westhill to find the old man with a nearly severed finger. In his most courtly way he apologized for disturbing me. It was really not important, but it would be a kindness if I would drive him down to the doctor, since the blood was dripping all over the place and making an unpleasant mess.

On the way to Rattleford he remarked that it was strange that he had survived the hunting of so many types of big game scatheless; had come without injury through many a pig-sticking; had quelled riots; and tracked the most dangerous quarry in the world, man. Yet this present hurt was got at the unspectacular task of cutting firewood.

When he returned some days later from hospital old Robertson resumed his customary visits at morning coffee time, and told us

that he must leave; that he could no longer cope with the light
engine, the pumping, the sawing of firewood, and the hundred and
one tasks of a house and garden designed for half a dozen employees;
that it was a profitless profit to look after the exacting demands of
pigs and fowls so that their income might help meet the overheads
of too large an establishment. In short, that he was too old a dog to
learn new tricks. He would go away to the ready-made amenities
of a small flat. After all, he would have the memories of a long and
eventful life to crowd about him for company.

Thus old Robertson gave up the lease of Westhill, and put up
his chattels for sale. Tessa went to the auction. She goes to all
within reach, and has returned with Dresden cups, wicker chairs,
galvanized wire netting, carpet underfelt, ornamented fireside tiles,
and home-made jam. This time she bought an ark for some of
Cable Street Joe's growing fowls. The children, of course, were
delighted at the news until we explained that it had no connexion
with early Biblical characters and the fauna of the time, and would
not, therefore, be launched in the fish-pond.

Tessa had more to say about the sale. The Topgoods had been
there, and had brought The Machine to auction. They were as
smart as ever, but during the two years since that day on which they
had sat on our veranda making mental notes of its dimensions, we
had noticed with each encounter that they were tiring. It appeared
that they were negotiating for a cabin cruiser, and that they proposed
to make it their home. As they said, a garden was of no value unless
its demands allowed you time to stroll through it or sit in it. A house
was no comfort if under its roof it offered only the sleep of exhaustion. They reckoned that there would be few domestic tasks in a
cruiser which could not be performed without more bodily movement than a long stretch. As an earnest of their determination to win
freedom, The Machine was for sale.

Tessa told us that she had considered buying it, but that Rachel
Hawkins, our near neighbour who had given us the female cat
Pandy and sold us Primrose and her sisters, was keen to purchase.
Thus it seemed that we should be able to borrow The Machine for
use without having to buy it. This is the most satisfactory sort of
rural arrangement.

It is my belief that the two women doctored the pawl and ratchet which held the clutch out of engagement. At any rate when one of a group of other interested customers pulled the starting cord The Machine moved smartly out of its shed by itself. Since the cutter-bar was attached, and the knives were oscillating greedily, it carved a path through the crowd until it stalled itself against the first immovable obstacle.

This depressed the bidding as when a horse savages its attendant in a sale ring, and Rachel bought The Machine for a song.

I believe that there must have been some bond of sympathy between The Machine and me. When first I saw it in Topgood's outhouse the Colonel had eyed it as he must often have eyed a wily defaulter who looked as if he might get the better of him. Now, a couple of days after the acquisition, Rachel Hawkins telephoned to say that she felt rather badly about having let Tessa stand aside in the bidding. She felt that, as I was the only person who had made full use of The Machine, she ought not to have been so selfish as morally to deter Tessa from buying. I might have it at the price she had given. Provided, that is, that I would fetch it.

I had already heard, through Bert Westmacott, that Rachel's gardener had had a similar experience to Bert's own at his first essay to handle The Machine. And that when he did in the end learn the knack of distracting its attention from the bushes he found its guidance and manipulation exhausting. I understood that Rachel must choose between her gardener and it.

And so inevitably, as if its inanimate iron will had so determined, the iron gardener came to Shallows.

We were not quite so brash in our purchase as people thought. Since my first taste of The Machine at unorthodox lawn levelling, I had felt that some implement of this sort might replace Bert when his ditching and human bulldozing was done. In that interval we had invited several eager implement agents to test their champions against the defences of our wilderness. The agents came confident of success. They unloaded the champions, gay in fresh war-paint, eager to try their assortment of clean, bright weapons on our jungle.

The result was always the same. We would suggest a little

ploughing on whatever vegetable patch Tessa had most recently been worrying Bert and me to dig. The salesman would attach his plough and move briskly to the tilting ground. Confidence would ebb as the couch-grass and the meandering roots of distant shrubs laid hold of the share and wound themselves around the coulter, angry at disturbance. As often as not the groaning machine would sink suddenly, and with an air of finality, into some soft spot which roofed a waterspring.

Bert, always a sceptical spectator at these events, would say without care for the salesman's feelings:

"Have 'un out o' there, so's I can get at patch with th'old spade." Having 'un out was not always easy, even though the models in which we were interested were the small types with engines of one or one-and-a-half horsepower. It is never easy to lift a mulish-tempered object out of a bog in which the lifters are sinking at a rate proportionate to their efforts.

We would renew hope in the demonstrators by saying that they were not to worry about the ploughing. Let us try out the cutter-bar. We were fair-minded enough not to suggest the wood, but set the tractor at some of the nearer bramble-brakes. All of these were shot through with sapling oaks, mountain ash, hazel, and syca-more, since every seed of tree or plant seemed to take root at Shallows. Nature has become used to sowing broadcast ten thou-sand seeds that one may survive all hazards. The trouble is that Nature does not realize that she may relax her reproductive efforts in our garden.

The bramble-brakes pursued harassing tactics. They would allow the cutter-bar to slice a road deep enough to bring the operator inside the perimeter. Whereupon the standing brambles to either side would tumble into the cleared space, enveloping man and tractor. If the man was wise he waited till Bert brought his long-handled bill-'ook to cut him loose. Some demonstrators, however, persisted with the attempt, thrashing about in the lacerating vines like panic-stricken rabbits in purse-nets. When we dragged them out, bleed-ing and exhausted, we would have to cut the tractors free. The tough, fibrous bramble stems would be entwined round every pro-tuberance of the frame and engine, and would have wound themselves about the turning axle until they had in the end stopped its revolution.

The failure of so many marques of tractor to do their work properly at Shallows was not all to be blamed on their designers, for they were being asked to do more than was reasonable. They would have performed well enough on normal, made gardens, but ours was abnormal and unmade. At least the demonstrations taught us the points of a small tractor, as horse-copers know a horse.

There is little to choose between the power-units, which are supplied to the tractor manufacturers by various reliable proprietary engine makers. The units have in common reliability, simplicity, and economy, for Britain has much skill in this field. The variations between marques lie largely in two less determinate factors: ease of tool changing, and ease of handling.

It is essential to buy a design which allows quick switches from one implement to another, for the average tractor will work plough, ridging plough, disc harrows, cultivators, rototillers, hoes, cutter-bar and lawn-mower. The power take-off will run a saw-bench or a hedge-trimmer. Some tractors will carry a tipping hopper in front to do the work of a barrow. Some tow a trailer. It is frustrating to have all these devices at hand, but to have difficulty in changing from one to the other.

A gardener's problem is not that of a farmer. A farmer may take half a day to set up an implement on his grown-up tractor, but then he often runs for a week or two without need to change.

The gardener, however, may in the same day wish to run the lawn-mower over the short grass, put the cutter-bar through the rough, earth up the potatoes with the ridging plough, and hoe between the cabbages. In fact, he must be a quick-change artist. Often, we found, the tool mounting designs would not allow him to be.

Some of the tractors, too, were a little clumsy. At the end of a row, perhaps, it was difficult to clear plough or cultivators from the ground in order to make a turn. Often the turn itself was not easy in the restricted headland of a vegetable plot. And our plots were indeed restricted by the wall of vegetation which hedged them in. They were more like the hopeful clearings of a Far Eastern jungle than the kitchen gardens of Britain.

After each trial we made comparison with The Machine of Topgood, and never did we fail to give it best for speed and ease of toolchanging. It was light enough to lug single-handed from a swamp or out of one of Bert's unfilled ditches. The only drawback had been its balance, for on our uneven ground its central ribbed drum gave it but precarious poise, and on rough ground both it and its handler, if he were a determined fellow, were likely from time to time slowly to fall over sideways together.

Just before Rachel Hawkins telephoned to ask us to remove The Machine before her gardener removed himself, we had heard that The Machine's makers were issuing a set of parts to convert their tractor to pneumatic tyres. This, it seemed, would cure its only fault.

Rachel, no doubt, thought us neighbourly to accept her offer as promptly as we did.

Bert Westmacott's original week's work had extended to a couple of years. Now his underground water-courses were completed; rough sods had been skum, and the bare earth resown; together we had tackled many jobs which could not readily have been done single-handed. It was a pity that, though his energy could change the face of the landscape, he could not heal the scars by planting and tending. Delicate seedlings were treated as if they were fencing-posts.

"What's tu worry? You can stuff they sorts of titchy things in arse end up. 'Twon't do 'em a bit o'harm."

Perhaps it was as well that Bert had this failing. Had he had the delicate touch of a Russell, no doubt he would have remained one more week to prick out the seedlings from the seed bed, and still have been with us yet another two years hence.

The Machine, transformed by its rubber-tyred wheels, took on the very sorts of work at which Bert had been so willing. It replaced the spade with the plough; the scythe and sickle with the cutter-bar; the rake with disc harrows. It even hoed for us—an operation at which Bert could never be trusted, since he was likely to scuffle down the lines of seedlings, but leave unharmed the weeds between them. Of course, there is no substitute for hands in the garden; for the tireless individual touch which earns the title of 'green

G

fingers.' The title is not earned by a quality miraculously given to a few, but by that infinite capacity for taking pains which is in every one, and used by so small a number. The employed gardeners of a decade or two ago were a vocational class who have been killed by the laws of economics, for it no longer pays to expend that dispro-portionate extra amount of labour to gain the small betterment of results which attain perfection. In the shortfall of this present day the germs of retrogression are bred.

When old Robertson told us that he was going to leave Westhill we acquired our only garden statue. My introduction to it had been made accidentally when I had been searching for a vast and spooky plant which the old man had told me of. I had heard tell of a gunnera at Westhill, and, guessing that this was it, went over to see whether I could recognize it, so that later in the year I might transplant a crown to our own wood.

Old Robertson had led me to the edge of his jungle, and I had gone into it alone, bending double along the bed of a stream which gave me a wet path. It was a gunnera right enough; a vast specimen, its rhubarby leaves, big as sunshades, held on fleshy, hairy stems which sprang upward and outward from a common base; but my eyes were held by a seated figure, half-turned from me, gazing down-stream. So lifelike was the figure, quiet as is one who is sad and seeks solitude, that I stopped involuntarily for a few moments, before going up silently to look closer. It was an exquisite Pan who sat on the stone tree-stump. There were a couple of rabbits at his feet, and one lay sprawled across his knees. A delicate hand held the reed pipes.

Pan was not playing, but was in a rather melancholy reverie. In his face and attitude was all the sadness of one conceived by a mortal of an Olympian sire; a sadness grown from the loneliness of the half-world which such offspring must inhabit. Hermes had had his Arcadian delight with Dryope, but she, when she saw the strange and faun-like babe, abandoned him. Pan had grown up with the streams and winds, the trees and grasses, for companions. The spirit of wild life was his.

Yet even an earthbound godling must in the end need deeper com-panionship than the dumb and the inanimate. It was an unhappy day when Pan glimpsed Syrinx, and loved her, for she was a nymph whose emotions were unawakened. She fled from his beseeching hand, whether half desirous of capture or not we shall never know, for when her flight was checked by the water of the river Ladon Pan did not have the opportunity to prove her willingness or distaste. Syrinx turned into a clump of rushes in his arms.

Pan fashioned his pipes from these very reeds, which is the reason, perhaps, why his music is so haunting and perplexed.

Once again Pan was stirred to a love beyond the ordinary by the beauty of Pitys. She too showed him how swiftly she could run, but in her case it was no more than a playful and probably inflamatory gesture, for women change little in character, and have always stayed constant to the deceptions men have insisted upon. On the edge of a cliff Pitys turned eagerly enough to Pan, now that the precipice gave the excuse for surrender. But Boreas, the North Wind, perhaps jealous, perhaps with his customary ill manners, buffetted the nymph over the edge. She fell before the eyes of distracted Pan. A pine-tree grew from the place among the rocks where her broken body lay, and her robbed lover clambered down to break off twigs to make for himself a crown whose sharp needles would remind him of her.

Unhappiness must find a solace, and now Pan's music became more moving than ever it had been. The birds and beasts, the nymphs, fauns, and dryads of Arcady, were bewitched by it; and the trees and long grasses whispered it from one to the other in widening echoes.

It was not surprising that Midas exclaimed one day that Pan's music was finer than Apollo's; nor was it surprising that Apollo acted as would have that other intolerant god, the Jehovah of the Old Testament. He demanded a contest; an Olympian Eisteddfod, with Midas as Adjudicator. When Midas gave the crown to Pan Apollo was so angry that the audience must have feared thunderbolts, but in the end the god restrained himself, being content to remark that Midas must indeed have the ears of an ass to hear so falsely. The unfortunate king was immediately so afflicted literally, becoming an unheeded warning to critics.

The Pan who sat in his hidden place beside old Robertson's

stream was gentle, cynical, bitter, and half-happy. He epitomized the compounded emotions of living.

I was so taken with him that when old Robertson told us he was going to leave Westhill I made an offer, which was accepted, and Pan rode home to Shallows in my new pneumatic-tyred wheel-barrow. I say that he rode home, for home Shallows was to him from the very start.

There was a flat ledge, backed by lichened boulders, beside the waterfall at the lower end of the long lily-pond. Osmunda fern and red and white astilbes partly screened the ledge, and saxifrages carpeted the ground. Here Pan sat, half turned to look up the pool and beyond it into the wood.

The children were very young when Pan came to Shallows, and even Louise had at that time but a sketchy idea of the myths. Certainly she had not heard much of Pan worship. I was superstitiously surprised, therefore, whenever I passed by Pan's new resting-place, to find him usually freshly garlanded. Sometimes there were flower-chains about his neck, sometimes berries laid on his lap, and sometimes, on hot days, he was shaded by a hat of water-plantation leaves.

This attention was given surreptitiously for some reason which I have never discovered, and it was only by chance glimpses over a long period that I discovered that both children independently were paying service to the wistful newcomer.

Was their uninstigated practice pagan instinct? Or was it that the genius of the small statue so appealed to their tenderness? If knowingly they made offerings to Pan, then they were but recognizing the sylvan god, the spirit of deep woods and swift waters.

CHAPTER EIGHT

*Turbary and venville—Marauders from the moor—The hungry
gap—Recipes of a Swiss chef—Nettle beer—Dandelions*

WE had felt from the first that the garden should, and could,
do something towards earning its keep. Yet it seemed unwilling. Direct or indirect disasters fell upon us as fast as we tried
to coerce the ground into commercial production. It did not seem
to grudge us a bite to eat for ourselves—in fact it fed us quite well
—but any planned surplus of production was ruthlessly slashed.
It was as if the garden was prepared to do its duty by us, but was
not going to be put upon.

Its main defence against exploitation was a passive resistance
derived paradoxically from its fertility. Everything grew which
nature cared to seed upon our soil. Sycamore spinners burrowed
into the earth; every acorn split and sprouted—except those eaten
by Harry George Pengelly's active pigs; every individual seed of the
explosive cypress magazines took hold, as did those of thuyas; the
drifting parachutes of dandelion seed, light as the lovers' sighs which
sometimes blow them, formed each their root; flowers, from ragged
robin and foxglove to convolvulus and tropæolum, struggled for
Lebensraum. Among these many scores of competitors were our
vegetables and soft fruits.

Thus the very fertility limited the area of dug garden whose
alien growths we could control. We did, however, manage to rear
very good crops on our necessarily small patches, and would look
forward to some delicious meals for ourselves, even though we
had nothing to sell to offset our rates and property taxes. At
this stage of anticipation the Dartmoor beasts have always made
their appearance.

The farms on and around the moor have rights of turbary and
venville. That is, they may cut turf and graze stock on Dartmoor.

Few cut the turf, but many abuse the grazing. The right of venville allows a farmer to summer as much stock on the moor as his
farm is capable of wintering when the time comes to drive them
down below. In the immediate post-War years government subsidies were aimed at the encouragement of hill breeds of cattle and
sheep. These payments did some public good on upland farms
proper, but little on those farms whose hill grazing was common
ground. On the true upland holding a farmer would never over-
stock his land to gain a catchpenny subsidy for a year of two at the
expense of the health of his flocks and herds and the deterioration
of his grassland.

But the moor is common. Everybody's business was nobody's
business when it came to limiting the numbers of beasts, which
were so many cash bonuses to their various owners. So long as
high subsidies prevailed the moor was grossly overstocked. In
fact, where sheep were concerned, the combination of subsidy and
high wool prices made it worth a shepherd's while to let his ewes
die of old age in a bog, rather than at proper drafting age in an abat-
toir. It was unfortunate in such cases that it was the crows who got
the meat, not the public who provided the funds for the subsidy.

It was also unfortunate for Tessa and me that the moor was overstocked, for the questing beasts on the fringe tended to be pushed
outward and downward. They were hungry, hardy, and contemp-
tuous of man and his works. Our fences at Shallows meant no
more to them than a playful obstacle; a constitutional before the
banquet.

What annoyed us most was that we had encouraged animal
visitors during our first winter. Rachel Hawkins' and Harry
George Pengelly's pigs had cleared up the annual layer of acorns
for us. Also several groups of ponies, and young store bullocks
and heifers, did some useful work on the long, dead grass between
the groups of shrubs. Furthermore, the children were thus introduced to pastoral hazards under our rescuing hands.

By the time our second winter had come round, so far from
giving encouragement to the attractive ponies and polled black
cattle and the comical pigs, we would have preferred to dig pitfalls
for them, complete with sharpened stake at the bottom.

The first quarrel was over some new potatoes. Tessa had taken great trouble over these, whose cultivation was her first vital step towards spiritual rusticity. She had sprouted the seed in a dark place. She had jeopardized the serenity of our marriage by an insistence little short of nagging on the preparation of a plot for them. I dug it for her in ground still frosted under a slush of melting snow. It was not an agreeable task.

That first spring was the pattern of English seasons. It was warm, and besprinkled by showers from a celestial watering-can with a fine rose on the spout. The potatoes flourished in their virgin patch, where the soil, bursting with accumulated virtue, was as eager for consummation as a spinster. Although they were at a thousand feet above the sea, Tessa's early potatoes were ahead of any we had news of, or peered over hedges at, down in the Teign valley. I earthed them up. They flowered, and one evening we decided that next day we would have our first dishful for lunch. It was a splendidly extravagant decision, for we knew that the potatoes would still be the expensive size beloved by gourmets. But still, as Tessa said, the sweat and tears of rural life must surely be allowed to offer compensation once in a way—if only by raising the vegetable standard at one meal.

On the morning of the appointed day I awoke earlier than usual. I had become well accustomed to the splatter of the waterfall a few yards from the south windows of our bedroom; and the dawn chorus of the multiplied descendants of the Little Kinglet birds, which was deafening. It was not these customary sounds which had awakened me, but some other noise. It was, my waking brain told me, not an unprecedented noise, but it was not an everyday one in the garden, and its sounding at this time was antagonistic to another thought struggling towards my consciousness.

The subliminal mind is more wonderful than a card-index. It is quite as wonderful as those Hollerith machines which can, for example, file the particulars of ten thousand people, and at the push of a button drop into your lap a list of those with red hair and three children; who are non-smokers and non-swimmers, but excel at accountancy and play bowls.

My subliminal did not have so spectacular a task to perform

that early morning. It just whispered urgently: "Pigs and potatoes. Your lunch is gone."

I was out in a flash in pyjamas and gumboots. I rounded the house at speed, and came abruptly upon the devastation of the potato patch. The rows so neatly banked at such labour, the ground so hardly won from bog and couch and bramble, was a torn travesty of a garden; a miniature of a shell-torn Flanders plain. The young haulms were uprooted to the last plant; their fruit had been nosed out to the last one. Two vast, waggling Wessex Saddleback behinds were swaying contentedly away through the fringing rhodo-dendrons. Their owners grunted to one another in the comfortable tones of those who have not only done a good morning's work before others are out of bed, but have enjoyed the doing.

I pursued the robbers through the shrubs, across a stream, and into the wood. Here they had the advantage of me, for I became immobilized in the brambles, and got but little satisfaction at hear-ing the two swine squeal now and then with pain as they tore a way to safety.

I extricated myself, and made a detour to the open side beside the bridle-path, up which clear way I ran, being in time to see the two sterns each give an indignant flourish as one followed the other through a hole in the fence. This was the rickety fence between us and the bridle-path, into which we had been assured no beast ever prowled, since the ends were sealed at lane below and moor above.

My interest in seeing what direction the marauders would take was because both were strangers to me. They were not the Large Whites of Harry George Pengelly, nor the nondescript sows of remote Berkshire ancestry of William Yeo on our other side.

The pigs nipped across the bridle-path with that deceptive swift-ness of their species, outdistancing the billet of wood which I bowled after them, burst through the other fence, and melted away among the trees of Rachel Hawkins' copse. I remembered now that Bert had told me her up yonder had gone and bought a couple of fancy gilts what'd like enough eat her out of house and home. Not at this rate, I reflected. It would be us who were eaten out.

It was Tessa who later telephoned to Rachel, a catch in her throat. Rachel was most upset, for she had often suffered herself from such outside depredations. She offered us free digging from a small field which she had planted with potatoes. Later on we did go once or twice to lift a half-hearted bucketful, but there was no pleasure in the work. The bucket did not hold the fruit of our own labour, nor were its contents stolen. Thus neither of the two primitive grounds for satisfaction in achievement were given.

What was given, however, was the opportunity to exercise the primitive blind persistence which has pushed us all out of the primeval slime.

Tessa went on planting in the little patches which Bert or I made ready for her. She planted all the usual seeds, and quite a few of the unusual. However, if it was not pigs, it was ponies, if not ponies, bullocks. The beasts sensed a ripened crop. Sometimes they scrambled like cats up the vertical bank of the lane, and burst through the dense holly-hedge which was as daunting as the spikes of a dragon's back; sometimes they came in through the wood, thrusting their heads under the ancient barbed wires which separated us from the ground of William Yeo, and thus lifting the old posts out of the ground; sometimes they lurked round a bend of the lane, patiently awaiting the odd few minutes in a day when the drive gate might be left open.

The moorland farmer, who is cunning if not intelligent, had three lines of defence against all threats.

The first was an appeal to good-neighbourliness.

"Us 'as all got to get along together best us can."

This aphorism was unilateral in application, and was only accepted by newcomers. Its soothing effect was ephemeral, and the red-faced men of the moor were soon forced back on number two. This defence was a denial that they were in any way responsible for the doings of their beasts, and that if the animals had destroyed a season's garden crops in a matter of minutes, then the garden was improperly fenced. An addition to this defence was a vague remark that 'twas a good thing they heifers had managed to break they cloches without cutting theirselves, else might have to be talk of compensation.

But, as in all wars, experience was rapidly gained on Dartmoor. The newcomer soon learned to rejoin that it was no man's duty to fence against the marauding beasts of others. The owner was responsible for the control of his stock. The newcomer, too, could add his little threat that, if the beasts had broken in out of the road, then there was an automatic fine levied upon the owner of beasts which strayed upon the highway.

The final position upon which the moorland farmer makes his last stand is that of sympathy. 'Tis a praper hard life herding they old beasts out along Dartmoor. A man can't forever be a-watching for to see they didn't get down off moor into folk's gardens. Anyway, they motorists were beggars for a-leaving open of t'moor gates.

In fact, there is little enough management applied to the stock which grazes Dartmoor. The attention given does not begin to compare with that lavished in other far more rugged and difficult upland areas: in Wales, for instance; in Cumberland and Westmorland; and along the chain of the Pennines.

By the time the last position is reached the newcomer has become an old-timer. He details the moor gates in the neighbourhood and says that the farmers should press the council to put in cattle grids, and that if the council were unwilling the farmers themselves should offer to do the job. The beasts could not then stray, the old-timer points out; and adds that it would not therefore be necessary to consider the impounding of wantons.

At the mention of a pound, the moor man flinches and looks reproachful like a cleric who overhears bad language. 'Tisn't neighbourly talk, and 'tisn't right to punish a beast for following his nature given him by God. The suggestion of redress is thus shown to be an impiety.

The old-timer refuses to be drawn into a theological discussion, beyond a reference to the wrathful Deity of the Old Testament, a patriarch who undoubtedly knew the customs where flocks and herds were involved, and who would certainly have laid down the principle of an eye for an eye; a broccoli for a broccoli.

'Twas a rare shame, but us didn't grow them things much, hereabouts. However, for to make sure there be no hard feelings, us'll drop in a sack of something to make up for that plot of vegetables what was eaten up. The sack usually remains as nebulous as a good resolution, though we did just once receive one from William Yeo as heart-balm for the loss of three months' supply of spring cabbage.

There were eight field turnips in the bottom of the sack.

This particular loss was a serious one, for Rattleford, like most country districts, knew a wide hungry gap through late winter until spring growth was in full flush. Rural greengrocers do not buy more than they must from the big wholesalers of the cities, but rely largely on local production. The retired senior officers in our district did their best to meet the demand, but none of them was sufficiently professional in this new career to offer very much early in the season. Indeed, they all appeared on the roads with vegetable-laden shooting-brakes as spontaneously and simultaneously as a hatch of may-fly. The cunning traders of Rattleford interpreted this activity as symptomatic of glut, and paid the producers accordingly. The price to the consumer, however, remained at the scarcity level of hungry-gap days.

Thus, when William Yeo's bullocks ate our spring cabbages in February not even a display of money could replace our loss from the resources of Rattleford. It looked as though we must accept the risks of scurvy and pimples until our own spring crops matured. We were fairly sure that William Yeo's compensation of eight turnips did not contain any of the right sort of vitamins to combat these ills, and that, even if they did, eight of them would not provide a large reservoir of protection for four of us.

Tessa made a few trips to the turnip-field from which William Yeo had extracted his offering, and plucked the green leaves from the crowns of the roots. These boiled up into green vegetables, which, if dull, satisfied Tessa's dietary conscience. Unfortunately, William turned his Scotch sheep into the field, and Tessa found the competition too much for her.

One day, during this desperate period, I came upon Tessa in the outhouse which had been designated a stable by the vendors of Shallows. I knew that something important was in the wind, for she was kneeling beside the leather trunk in which she kept suovenirs and scraps of literary material, any of which might one day be useful. The floor of the stable was already covered with a representative selection of human ingenuity and written knowledge. There were dress patterns; snapshots and negatives sallow with age; outmoded dance programmes with pencils dangling from coloured threads; newspaper clippings of hints for removing ink-stains, making apple jelly, or constructing hayboxes; clippings to commemorate odd facts such as the incidence of blue babies or odd events such as a Shakespearean production in modern dress; neat bundles of tweed patterns, moth eaten; travel folders; bus tickets; old bank books; bundles of cancelled cheques; shoe-boxes filled with letters; satchels of lavender as dead as the past; and school exercise-books.

It was a particular one of these exercise-books that Tessa sought, but although she had already found it when I discovered her in the shed after breakfast, she did not come away until lunch. She remained beguiled by the magpie collection of mementoes in the trunk, just as traditionally a fish-and-chip addict reads avidly the newspaper in which his meal is wrapped.

The exercise-book which Tessa recovered from limbo was filled with cooking recipes written in French by a juvenile hand. But if the calligraphy was immature, the standard of French taught by that Swiss school was so high that both of us were reminded of how much we had forgotten. The recipes were those of the school's Swiss chef, whose memory Tessa revered, and had been imparted to the young ladies during the curriculum.

It was clear that the chef had exploited to the full the Continental use of herbs and the growths which the Anglo-Saxon dismisses as weeds, useless to the stomach and detrimental to the land. The uses of the weeds were described in stilted French more suited to the disciple of an Academician than a cook, though the pomposity of phrase in fact paid tribute to the importance with which most Continental races invest the culinary artist.

I was delighted to learn later on that two of the most favoured raw materials were the nettle and the dandelion. This was indeed fortunate, for these plants were in plentiful supply at Shallows.

The children and I were at first ignorant of Tessa's precise designs, for I had not bothered to read deep into the old exercise-book. It was with some concern, therefore, that I listened to the children's breathless description of her eccentric actions. It appeared that their mother, of whom they were very fond, was knee deep in the big nettle patch by the gentle holly clump where Johanna had a private den. It might be that she was fulfilling Johanna's repeated request that the nettles be destroyed, but it was surely going to be a long business if performed with the kitchen scissors. It occurred to the children that I would do the job more efficiently with the long-handed sickle, and that in any case their mother should be soothed and gently led back to the house for a nice lie down.

At first sight the performance was odd. The children had fairly accurately described Tessa's actions. She was not, however, venting wholesale destruction upon the nettle-bed, but rather was snipping here and there with the selective air of a lady gathering roses. The nettle heads upon which she decided were dropped one by one into a white enamel pail, which was hung upon a convenient branch of the gentle holly-tree.

In answer to my careful inquiries, put delicately as a doctor might to an amnesia subject, Tessa answered that she was gathering a bucket of greens to fill the hungry gap which had been opened yet wider by the recent incursion of the Dartmoor beasts.

I understood then the reason for the secretiveness of the operation; like most housewives she was plagued by the remarks of any of her family who came upon her during the preparation of food. She was tired of the startled remark, bitten off at the end lest it give offence or bring retribution: "Oh! Are we going to eat that!"

Undoubtedly on that morning it had been her intention to present the nettles as a delicious *plât accompli* at table, and laughingly to brush aside our questions until we had tasted and expressed delight. Now, poor girl, there was nothing for her to do but snip doggedly on, while we watched gloomily, the children holding hands in mutual defence.

At the finish we trailed along behind her towards the house, with me carrying the pail, looking, I suppose, like victims marching in procession to dig their own graves. On the way I noticed several inverted flower-pots set here and there, and began to repri-mand the children. Tessa interrupted to say shortly that it was she who had thus placed the pots. I was apprehensive of provoking her, but, overcome by curiosity, asked her whether it was some kind of slug trap. She answered very abruptly, that she was blanching dandelions.

The nettles duly appeared at table. The dish closely resembled creamed spinach. Gingerly, and with many a sidelong glance, the children and I helped ourselves to a spoonful apiece, spreading the concoction about on our plates in order to make our helping look a large one. We were astonished to find that the nettle was delicious, and Tessa expanded in a deprecating sort of way as with cries of joy we helped ourselves to more and asked eagerly when we might have some again.

Had Tessa's new dish been a proprietary product, an advertising copy-writer could have drawn a really nauseating series of his little success-story pictures, this time straight from life.

From then on nettles became a regular dish in the household during the early part of the year. The plants came at a most convenient time in the vegetable calendar, for not even a garden secure from pests has much to offer in February. That which it has is either dull or forced; and somehow I feel that a forced growth has not the valuable health properties of a plant which has matured without artificial aid. After the sunless damp of a British winter the body needs young, naturally grown green food, and no vitamin pill will make up its lack. Old country folk have long realized this need, and have eaten the nettle, though without much imagination in the cooking, as I remember during my boyhood in Wales. Indeed, the wartime Ministry of Food recommended the nettle as a supplement to our rations. "Boil as for cabbage," they said. The English way of maltreating greenstuff renders it fit only for application as a poultice, and the nettle, thus threatened, sulked for the duration of hostilities.

Tessa's nettle dish was so delectable, and became so highly esteemed, that she rationalized its production, and developed an ancillary or two. She came to work upon what might have been termed a basic bucket. In other words, she found that a bucketful of nettle tops would produce three different dishes, each enough for the four of us.

She took at first two-thirds only of her bucketful, part of which amount was destined to be the dish which had first captivated the family. This, however, was no dank mess of limp green-stuff. The production was not straightforward. Firstly, as I found by observation through the kitchen window, Tessa tenderly rinsed her nettle tops under the cold tap, then boiled them in salted water. The first time I saw a cauldronful I thought that she was making enough for us and Bert Westmacott's two baconers, but within minutes the bulk shrank to domestic proportions.

When the boiling was done Tessa strained the nettle water into a crock; then put the green-stuff through the mincer, sending after it, through the machine, with tears, a couple of onions.

It was now that the delicatesse of the Swiss school chef began to reflect itself in the pupil. Tessa began to cook the minced onion and some crushed garlic with a little margarine in a pan. When the onion was golden brown she added nettle water and flour, and cooked the mixture until it thickened. Then she put in the minced, cooked nettles, dashed in some seasoning, stirred the lot up together, and let everything simmer for a while.

The untutored weeds which had surrounded Johanna's gentle holly den were as transformed as would be a savage in the habiliments of Royal Ascot—though the garlic touch suggests Longchamps.

It may be remembered that two-thirds of Tessa's basic bucket has been thus treated. A half of this cooked amount becomes a dish for the immediate meal, but the other half is set aside. On the morrow it is whipped up with two or three eggs, and put into the oven to become a timbale.

The last third of the basic bucket lies still untouched, but the astral projection of the Swiss chef is equal to it, though it is likely that he now browses among beds of celestial dead-nettles. This last part becomes the basis of two soups. The first, which the children enjoy particularly noisily, is Potage Valaison, named after the Swiss canton of Valais. Tessa cooks up together in margarine another of her lachrymatory minced onions, together with two or three sliced potatoes. She adds a fistful each of chopped dandelion leaves, nettles, and wild sorrel. She powders the whole conglomeration with flour, then pours in stock until she has the right bulk to feed the hungry mouths for which she is responsible.

The only other soup formula which her Swiss chef bequeathed to her produces Potage Vert-pré, which is a little different from the Valaison. For this delight you melt some margarine in a pan, as a substitute for the chef's butter, and add a handful of chopped cress, and another of either nettles or sorrel. You want to put in a little chopped chervil if you have any, otherwise parsley.

Cook the whole lot lightly in the fat; then pour in the stock, add the seasoning, and simmer for twenty minutes. Throw in a little tapioca, and cook on for another ten minutes. At the very last add a splash of milk.

These hedgerow recipes were undoubtedly much developed by those ranging Continental armies which cut their locust swathes across the European countryside for a millenium. Many a cantonment stewpot and many a lean bivouac mess-tin must have been enlivened and even enriched by the herbs of the *verts prés*. Those armies lived upon the countryside as parasites devour a defenceless host, and it was not until Napoleon began to defeat his enemies by the employment of what are now called logistics that a quartermaster system of supply was tentatively begun and looting was regularized by the requisition form.

Our discovery of nettles had been prompted, as are most discoveries, by hardship. It had, however, been the hardship of the hungry gap; as a precaution against a thirsty gap we tried our hands at nettle beer. This was not bad stuff, although I confess that as long as the house of Whitbread continues to brew I shall not forsake them—not even for the love of fermented nettle juice.

The beer is quite easy to make. You gather twenty pounds of young nettles—a quantity which devastates an extensive bed; —wash them, and cram them into a pan. Pour on two gallons of water, and add half an ounce of root ginger, four pounds of malt, two ounces of hops, and four ounces of sarsaparilla. Now let the whole lot boil for quarter of an hour. Meanwhile get ready another pan, and put a pound and a half of castor sugar into it. Strain in the boiled nettle liquid, and stir away until the sugar is melted.

Finally, you add an ounce of yeast, beaten up into a cream.

All this has powerful latent properties, as we found when we bottled our first brew as soon as fermentation began in the pan. Unwisely we rammed the bottle corks well home. Within twelve hours the beer began to do its work. In some instances it fired out the corks with great velocity, at which unexpected freedom immense volumes of foam welled forth from the bottles. If the corks were stubborn the powerful liquid burst the bottles themselves.

For a couple of days the house quaked under the irregular percussions, as a raided city is rocked by delayed-action bombs. We never knew when another bottle would go off, and all of us redeveloped that brittle insouciance which I had previously associated with bombs, artillery shells, or mortaring. Worse still, the larder, where I had thoughtlessly ranged the bottles, became hazardous of entry, and one sidled in and out very quickly with a tray held up as a shield.

However, at our second attempt we knew better and stored the stuff in an outbuilding. But this time I used screw-top bottles, and for several days left the stoppers but part screwed down. The deadly energy within the bottles could thus gain no firm purchase for its feat of strength, but dissipated its vital force past the loose stoppers. When the beer stopped work I tightened down, and we left the stuff to do its worst for three months.

Of course, true country people have long known of the value of the nettle as an anti-scorbutic, and of the efficacy of the formic acid injected by its sting in cases of rheumatism. Indeed, it is possible that the Romans deliberately introduced the nettle into this country, for it is not a native of Britain. I dare say that the bare nether limbs of the legionary, however hirsute, stiffened in the joints under the rigours of our island winters. Perhaps the nettle was used as a herbal remedy, applied externally.

We do know that the nettle was extensively employed in Rome in external application for less reputable purposes, and that it has been so used before and since in many countries. For chastisement of the lumbar region with a handful of sturdy plants has been proved an excellent stimulus to counter male impotence.

A curious plant is the nettle. Like the robin, it is only found about human dwellings or in the neighbourhood of man's works. At

H

Shallows, at any rate, we are glad enough of the nettle's proximity during the very early spring, for it is the first of the natural spring green to begin to rebuild the metabolism damaged by winter.

Nearly as early is the dandelion. We seem to have two sorts in our garden; one with broad leaves, like a cos lettuce; the other with narrow leaves, serrated at the edges. The narrow-leaved type is perfectly good, but we prefer the broad sort on the whole, and have noticed that it may be picked as late as June before it becomes over bitter. Dandelion leaves have a sharp, clean tang about them, and we served them as the Swiss chef recommended, either whole or chopped, with a French dressing. They make a particularly good appetizer taken thus with hot meals.

Tessa's flower-pot experiment turned out well. By the time her first blanched plants were ready we had been won over both to nettles and to green dandelion leaves, so that we were without prejudices from the start. The plants were the colour of young celery, and as crisp. We sliced them off just below the soil, and when our basket was filled the contents looked like a picking of blanched sea-kale.

Now that we have come to rely on these spring plants, and to look forward to their first appearance each year, we are posed a difficult garden weed problem, for if we eliminate the nettle and dandelion we do so at the expense of our table. In the end we have made the traditional compromise, and have left the two species to flourish in a few hidden, disreputable corners.

If any supercilious visitor does happen to break away from a conducted tour, and so comes across a waist-high nettle-bed, we can always explain that it is specially cultivated *Urtica edibilis*, very rare, and beloved of gourmets.

At the worst, the stranger will only have confirmed for him the rumour that Shallows is a madhouse.

CHAPTER NINE

*The wood and a plan for a kitchen garden—Tree-felling—The
man in the ulster—Treatment for horse-radish—A way through
the wood—Corduroy causeways and bridges—Clearing the plot—
Athelstan's misadventure—Sailor ploughman*

Our grounds at Shallows were shaped like a fat 'L.' The
horizontal limb in which stood the house and buildings
was slowly civilized by human and mechanical attentions. That is,
it was civilized as much as we wished it to be: the fallen timber was
removed for firewood, the brambles were discouraged by cutting,
and such nettle-beds as remained lived only by Tessa's clemency to
feed us in early spring. But the upright leg of our L was filled by
the wood, and for a long time remained savage, mostly impenetrable
and almost unexplored.

Yet we had always been sensible of the beauty of the wood,
though daunted by the thought of taming it as much as would be
necessary to enjoy it. We had made expeditions to its topmost
boundary by the route of the open ride beside the bridle-path to
the moor, and had once or twice forced a way here and there towards the centre.

There was a variety in our wood. We had seen a pair of immensely
tall pines; some horse-chestnuts; a trident-tree; holly in clumps,
and solitary hollies shaped like formal Christmas-trees; single,
symmetrical rhododendrons, and huge mounds of twenty-foot
bushes; alders as lofty and straight as the masts of a windjammer;
little hazel copses; and a score or two of oaks whose growth had not
run to trunks, but to an immense spread of branches. These oaks
were bearded with lichen, like a gathering of ancient wiseacres, and
big groups of the wavy-edged Devon fern sprang from the moss
in the forks between their huge limbs.

The bridle-path boundary began with a ten-foot rhododendron-hedge, and continued with fifty-foot thuyas which grew so closely that their frond-like foliage formed a screen as sleek and impenetrable as a pigeon's wing. Beyond the wall of thuyas the boundary was kept by hollies, supported here and there by massive oaks.

The upper edge of the wood ran with the contour of the swelling apron which fell from the moor. It was lined all the way by hollies and the fairy rowan, and between it and the open heather was the forestry plantation of infant conifers. The remaining long side, stretching down from the conifer plantation to the civilized parts about the house, was also marked by hollies and oaks. But this side was alive with the leap and gleam of the stream which had come to us in breathless haste from over the edge of the moor just above. The stream forked at fifty yards down, and a lesser branch bore off towards the centre of the wood, vanished within the huge clump of crimson rhododendrons, gathered strength from a spring or two, and reappeared nearer the house. Here it fed the lily-pool, then ran beside the bridle-path to join the fish-pond near the lane.

In the top bridle-path corner was the open space which we had seen with visionary eyes as our kitchen garden. It was open only by comparison with the thickest parts of the woods, for it was densely grown with young saplings: chestnut, hazel, ash, and alder, for the most part. The bracken was waist high, and all the vegetation was laced into a composite mass by brambles.

Shallows always gently forced us to courses of action which were not really of our own minds' instigation. The place hinted to us that Tessa's little allotment plots of vegetables were no longer quite the thing in the parts about the house, which were now fairly respectable. If we had ever intended, as we said we had, to make a proper kitchen garden up in the wood, then now was the time.

It is axiomatic that a country is as civilized as its communications. I saw that our wood could never be civilized by the presence of a garden unless there was easy access. True, a tractor could bucket its way up the bridle-path, and through a field gate in the topmost fence, but this route was widely divergent from the Shallows-garden beeline. It was not an acceptable route for a woman in a hurry to pick a couple of lettuces to please an unexpected guest. Clearly I must make a route through the wood, and while I was about it it might as well be good enough for both a wheel-barrow and The Machine.

A survey showed the need for two ten-foot bridges and one of six foot; for a causeway across ten yards of bottomless bog; for the firming of several long stretches of soft ground; and for the making of the last stretch into an acceptable gradient.

I thought about the task for several days, and came to the conclusion that it was more formidable than had been the levelling of the lawn. Tessa inquired from time to time when it was that I proposed to start, and I as often replied that one must not be hasty, since a major affair of this sort must be right from the inception.

A closer survey made during a really determined penetration of the jungle revealed that among the obstacles were several fallen trees and many dangling limbs, for which the great snows of 1947 had been responsible. I had the inspiration to put first things first, and told Tessa that before I began work we must carry out our timber plans.

We had long determined that we wanted to fell twenty-eight trees. The least wanted was a ninety-foot fir which towered from a base not ten feet from the sitting-room. It was so positioned that if it chose to fall to the prevailing south-westerly gales which lashed its top so wildly it would lie along the length of the house from end to end. Then we wished to remove several trees which overhung the fish-pond, filling it with leaves, and shading it in our imagination against the bright day when it would become a swimming-pool. Up in the wood were a few damaged trees, and a few which were crowding better specimens.

This last was my defence. It was useless to play with refinements in the wood until the timber men had done their worst, and gone.

Tessa accepted this excuse so trustingly that my conscience forced me to action. I wrote in turn to three Devonian timber merchants. In each case the procedure followed a familiar pattern. They thanked me for my letter, and their Mr So-and-so would have pleasure in calling on me shortly to make an offer for my standing timber. I suppose that the junior clerks who answered for their firms sighed with relief, and said to themselves that no one would have to do anything about that for a month, anyway.

A second letter from me was answered with varying ingenuity: Mr So-and-so was on holiday; was seriously ill; or simply busy. I gained the impression that the latter gentleman would have preferred severe illness.

I reminded my first firm several times over six weeks, and began at last to receive encouraging replies. Mr So-and-so was back, and was rapidly clearing his arrears of work. He could scarcely contain himself until the happy day when he would be free to look at my trees.

One day the voice which answered my telephone call was a strange one. I recounted the saga, and catalogued the broken promises and postponed arrangements.

"Well, don't 'ee worry, m'dear," said the voice soothingly. "'Tisn't no good for to expect us to come out up yonder. Us knew that straight away. Us hasn't got any of they little short timber-wagons what'll go round corners like they little sharp narrow ones up your lane. Us all knows your lane well through driving up on picnics like."

The unseen man used the tone of one who had done his best to keep me in the happiness of anticipation, but felt bound to say at last that it was not reasonable to expect him to keep up the illusion for ever.

I never learned whether the second firm's Mr So-and-so succumbed in hospital, although I did hear of his symptoms each time I telephoned. They seemed to me to get more and more dangerous, and I became increasingly diffident about asking when I might expect him to see my trees. Nothing sudden happened with this firm: we just drifted apart into the seemly silence appropriate to the neighbourhood of a death-bed.

It was a year or two later, apropros of something quite different, that I had reason to believe that the stricken Mr So-and-so was one and the same person as the man on the telephone.

I had learned wisdom when I came to tackle the third firm: the busy one. But with all my experience I found it difficult to obtain their definition of business. At first it was: "Well, give us a call next week, m'dear. Maybe things'll be a bit easier."

In the end I discovered that this game of telephonic plum-stones would not end on a 'this year,' or even a 'next year;' but probably on 'sometime,' and possibly on 'never.'

It was Harry George Pengelly who popped out of the ground one day to relieve my gloom as I stared at the unwanted scrub-trees around the fish-pond.

"You try Luke Fox over to Hollow Pasture," said Harry George. "For sure he'll shift they old trees out of it."

I knew that Harry and Luke were some kind of marriage connexions, and reckoned that Harry George might have sounded Luke out before making so sweeping a statement to me. Even so I was unprepared for the swift sequence of events. I telephoned Luke Fox's den in the middle of the Moor, and was told by some female that he would visit me at two o'clock on the following afternoon.

After lunch next day I was preparing to go to Exeter when I was astonished by the arrival of Luke at two precisely. He was a man as hard and gnarled as any lump of part-petrified bog oak preserved in the peat of the moor. He was grey-haired, hard-living, and hard-dealing, but he was a man I liked at once. He wore a suit of Glen Urquart tweed: the high-buttoned jacket was cut with tiny lapels and had skirts which flapped half-way down his thighs. His trouser legs were tight as a pair of stove pipes, and ended like jodhpurs at the uppers of wonderfully polished brown boots.

We forced a way into the wood, and old Luke turned a cold eye over the trees which I showed him. He was sparing of words, but scribbled a symbol or two in a notebook. There was a young man with him, equally silent, who, at a nod, slashed a blaze on each tree and wrote a number on the white exposed surface. At last we came back to the house, and I indicated the giant fir, our pride and fear. Old Luke was not impressed, but made his usual symbol.

He spent a couple of minutes with his hieroglyphics.

"Twenty-five pounds!" he said. "And start next Monday."

For once I did not haggle, so softened had my resistance become after the frustrations of my previous timber men. Indeed, I had feared that I might have to pay to have the trees felled and removed.

"Done!" I said.

At once Old Luke pulled out his cheque book, wrote one in my favour, raised his hat, and stumped off to his car, followed by his silent accomplice.

Quite a large gang turned up on the Monday. The men attacked the trees as if they had a personal grudge against them, and the whole property resounded to axe, saw, and the typical splintering crash of falling timber. The urgency of the gang was because old Luke Fox paid them according to the cubic footage of timber felled and cleaned.

The silent accomplice was present for much of the time, and he told me, in answer to a question, that his brother was in change of the operations. I tackled the brother about a certain point, but was in turn referred to the silent one who explained that it was a third brother whom I wanted. I found Tertius with a timber-wagon which he had manœuvered up the bridle-path and into the wood, and was told by him to ask his brother with the winch tractor. I gave up for the time being, and was glad to see Bert Westmacott, who, though working elsewhere now, always turned up when anything unusual was going on at Shallows. He explained about this great tribe of brothers.

"'Tis old Luke's boys, they be," he said. "Ten or a dozen he's got, beside a girl or two. 'Tis a rare old character, is Luke."

Bert had turned up that morning to see the big fir come down, for by country grape-vine he knew that it was to fall during the day. He was not a comfort to me.

"'Tis to be hoped sap's stopped running," he remarked, "else they'll never get saw to slide back an' fore. They firs are terrible sticky. Surely they dasn't leave tree half sawn through overnight. 'Twould crush house like match-box if wind off moor was to catch top of 'un."

I went off to assure myself that the gang was going to sink their professional pride and guy the tree with wire cable. But when I told Bert of this precaution he was not much impressed.

"I've seen they great old firs spin on their butts like little old tops," he said with dreamy relish, "and men dropping their tools and running for their lives, not knowing which way 'twould tumble. Cable ain't no good. If old tree spins 'twill wind cable round top till wire snaps like cotton. Likely back lash will catch some one too," he added, with the satisfaction of a music-hall addict who thinks he may see an unadvertised turn.

"Them cables," he went on, "'ll cut a man in half like they little wires the grocers used to have for slicing cheese."

Tessa now came out to watch the men who were making the first undercut with axes. She was fairly satisfied that the tree would not be felled across the house, but was much concerned about a group of young thuyas and two rhododendron clumps some of which would be obliterated if the tree deviated by more than a degree or two from the line which we had planned for it.

Bert Westmacott and the nearest posse of Luke's sons were mentally blind to this solicitude, for the shrubs were no more to them than 'they old bushes.' However, one of the few qualities the Devonian is quick to show is gallantry, and one and all assured Tessa that, whatever disaster befell house, linhays, or garage, all of which were within range of the eighty-foot tree, they little old bushes shouldn't be harmed a bit, m'dear.

More than once during that day I had misgivings about the giant fir. I felt like a one-man judge and jury who has had second thoughts after pronouncing verdict and judgment. It was not that I did not wish the tree away, for its needles blocked our rain gutters, its great branches threw a big area into gloom rather than shade, and it remained always an instrument with which a gale might destroy us. Yet the patient, laborious, and finally triumphant achievement of that fir-cone from whose puny womb the giant had sprung was not lightly to be destroyed. The autocratic impatience of man was about to humble in three parts of a day the dignity which nature had built over three-quarters of a century. The act was, I felt, a breach of decent manners.

By mid-afternoon the alternation of saw and wedge had tilted the trunk a little out of the upright, and now and again there came a groan from within the deep slice in the butt. The children, hand in hand, joined us to watch the last moments of the tree. They were not excited, but awed and sad, and I was glad that they felt so.

The fall began with no more spectacular warning than a hard, dry creak from the heart of the trunk. We looked up to the distant tip which fingered the sky for the last time. It cut a slow arc across the clouds, unhurried, as seemly and proper as had been the stabbed Cæsar, concerned that his dying should be done with imperial dignity.

They were long seconds as we watched the lingering fall, and listened to the drawn sigh of the boughs. The mighty, splintering crash took us by surprise, and we stood still for quite a while in the silence which closed in behind the echoes. The tree lay to a foot where old Luke's sons had willed it, and Tessa's shrubs had been no more than gently brushed by the tips of the boughs and gently stirred by the wind of the fall.

I was surprised to hear a polite voice beside me say:

"I hope that I am not intruding on you."

Tessa and I turned to see a stranger. He was a very tall man of some age, distinguished of face and spare of figure. He might have been a barrister, an architect, or perhaps—as a faint burr suggested—a Scottish laird. He wore very seasoned but expensive boots which laced half-way up the calf and a long garment which dim memory told me was an ulster. The ulster was weathered into the blue-green of lichen and had a vintage air, like the bouquet of old wine. The newcomer was holding his cap six inches above his head. We said "certainly not" to the fear of intrusion, and the cap was replaced, flat and perfectly straight, in the manner formerly *de rigueur* on the first tee at St Andrews among golfers of the old school.

I remarked that I had seen our visitor's back through the grocer's window, and from certain information vouchsafed to me when I had called in a few minutes later understood that he was our neighbour, the new tenant of Westhill.

The stranger opined that I was correct, sir, in my speculation, and that the name was Drummond. Meanwhile, might he inquire what I was doing with my timber, and whether in particular I had received a satisfactory price for the tree which had just been felled. I must excuse a curiosity which I might consider verged upon the unmannerly, but among other interests my humble servant numbered that of professional forester.

I knew now what would come. I knew that the low price which I had willingly accepted would be met with a "tut-tut" and what a pity that Drummond had not known sooner. One rarely recounts a deal to an acquaintance without being returned the half-sorrowful, half-reproachful reminder of what might have been had the acquaintance put one in touch with old So-and-so.

Drummond went one better. He audibly measured the cube of the tree by eye alone, and told me to the shilling what it was worth standing, felled in the round, and sawn into a variety of combinations of plank sizes. However, what was done was done. If in the future we required to know anything about arboriculture he would be at our disposal.

At that Mr Drummond raised his cap courteously and departed with measured strides, the veteran ulster lending him the dignity of a personage.

Shallows was in a sorry mess when the last timber-wagon left under escort of some of Luke Fox's sons. They had taken only the trunks of the trees, and the trimmings lay just where they had been cleaned off. The fish-pond was surrounded and part-filled with boughs. Much of the wood was choked with them. But none of the chaos measured with that where the big fir had lain. Some of the fir's boughs had driven deep into the ground; many were as thick as the stem of a young tree; all were interlaced with one another, so that one had always to search for the key branch.

I sawed and axed for a month before the tangle was clear, but at the end I had a fine stack of poles, whose trimmings had been burnt on a fire which had not gone out during the clearance. Tessa came to admire the fire after it had been going for a couple of weeks, and, in that deflationary manner peculiar to women, remarked that it was laid upon her only bed of horse-radish. As it happened, I may here have hit upon a new method of culture, for next spring our horse-radish roots were as large as parsnips, and the leaves grew to an unprecedented size.

However, at the time I was not to know of the edible Phœnix which would grow through the ashes of my fire, and to divert reproach drew Tessa's attention to the poles which would open up to her the route to her new kitchen garden. Quick to seize advantage, she suggested that I should begin to open it up at once, and now that Luke Fox had come and gone I could think of no ready excuse for delay.

The direct route to the garden was a diagonal laid from the bottom right-hand corner of the wood, to the top left corner where the clearance was to be made. There was plenty of work to be done over most of the way, but the only part which was not straight-forward hard labour lay at the start.

Access from the house to the start was by an existing wide track which ran through a high roofed tunnel formed by the overlapping greenery of rhododendrons on one side and young pines on the other. But the path dived suddenly down some steps to cross a stream just below the waterfall over which it poured out of the wood, whereas I required Tessa's garden route to run above the fall. It was here, where no less than three water-courses met in a bog, that the problem lay. One water-course was the perimeter ditch cut by Bert Westmacott during the long preliminaries of orchard-making; one came through from William Yeo's field beyond our side boundary; the other was our own main stream from the moor. Our new road must cross the lot, and also the seg-ments of bog through which they had carved a way.

In the end, the work went more easily than I had expected. I made first two firm strips across the two segments of bog which separated the streams. True, the bogs were nearly bottomless, but near by were many fallen and rotted trees which I fed corduroy-wise into the almost insatiable ooze.

Although it was now mid-winter, the children were strongly attracted by the alternation of mud and water, and spent most of their time with me, neglectful of their many other activities.

The bog was remarkable even in a neighbourhood whose bogs are sticky enough to catch escaped convicts and to hold them feebly wriggling like flies on a flypaper. Our bog was not only glutinous, but possessed a deep suction, like a thirsty haymaker. I only tried once to stand in it, and was forced to extricate myself by stepping out of my rubber boots to seek a solid footing in the bed of the main stream. The recovery of the boots was difficult, and was only achieved by kneeling in the stream and presenting a broad area of chest to the bog while I wallowed at each boot in turn. It was as well that I fell full length in the water when the second boot, with a noise like a three-dimensional osculation, came free unexpectedly, for the stream, though bitterly cold, was purifying.

I developed a technique in the building of my causeway, since it was essential to drop the logs exactly in their destined places. If they went awry their own weight of a hundredweight or so apiece combined with the boot-devouring suction to make them immovable. I had, therefore, to balance each log on my shoulder, and tote it along the stream bed, which was slippery but firm. Provided I did not fall over a boulder, I would come opposite the next spot to be filled, and letting one end of my log drop forward into my cupped hands, would toss it like a caber into the maw of the bog.

The children, of course, were pleased spectators of these upland games, and frequently experienced that acme of juvenile delight which is savoured when ignominious disaster trips an adult. However, I would have preferred to have continued in my lowly part of slapstick entertainer than to have passed to the next phase in construction. For no sooner was the bog sated with logs than the children swarmed across the stream and sprang to and fro on the causeway like mad castaways on a raft. Inevitably they sprang overboard at intervals, and must be rescued bootless and blackened.

We ought all to have suffered from pneumonia or pleurisy before the end of this period, but we caught not even a common cold.

I was by now corduroy-minded, and joined the causeways to each other in the middle, and to dry land at either end, by three corduroy bridges. In their skeleton state these bridges were but three pairs of very stout poles, once branches of the big fir, laid about six feet apart and spanning their respective waterways. Across them I proposed to lay short lengths as the actual roadway of the spans. Unfortunately, it took time to carry my cross-poles to the site, to saw them, and to lay them. In the interval the children tight-rope-walked along the main poles and crossed tropical, crocodile-infested rivers. It was fortunate that there were no saurians in the Shallows streams, or neither child would have remained undevoured.

I did not lay my cross-pieces at right angles to the main members of each bridge, but at a slight slant. This was in the best tradition of military construction, and was so designed that a wheeled vehicle, running squarely across, would not put the full weight of an axle on one cross-piece at the same time.

Tessa came out to view the first completed bridge and was puzzled by this slanting arrangement. I gave the explanation to her, and she made no comment. Later, however, I came upon her wheeling the barrow to and fro with the judicial air of a scientist. The experiment convinced her that no method of handling saved each cross-piece in turn from receiving the full weight. I agreed with her finding, and assured her that the design was not of advantage in the case of one-wheeled vehicles, but would come into its own when The Machine first disturbed the silence of the wood.

I levelled the causeway and the approaches to the bridges with fine gravel out of the stream, and we found ourselves able to set foot in the wood in ordinary shoes for the first time. But it was a small bridgehead we had won. In our pride we would bring friends to stand on the far bank of the main stream, but when we described to them the beauties which would unfold as our road was driven deeper and deeper towards its objective they made the soothing murmurs to which we were accustomed when describing our projects.

Yet the road progressed rapidly, with the children pressing on my heels as I levelled the hummocks into the hollows; tipped stone into the soft stretches, and smoothed them over with gravel; bridged the middle stream; and finally cut a grade aslant the last sharp rise to the shelf where the kitchen garden was to be.

We were a little disappointed with the results gained by our road. Here and there the children found that new dens were accessible, and Tessa caught glimpses of new shrubs and of a glade or two, but all I saw was blood and sweat. I saw the natural debris of twenty years; boughs and trees strewn by moorland storm and prostrated by moorland snow; a mat of bracken; bogs which had spread from choked water-runnels; and weaving through and under and above every obstruction were the Devon brambles, coiled like dannert wire, rooted at foot and at tip to trip a man, swarming up the living trees as well as along the fallen. Enough is enough, I thought. Let us for a time be content to travel to and from our kitchen garden without deviation, as jungle-dwellers trot the narrow tracks from village to village.

However, there was as yet no kitchen garden. Our road was like the fakir's rope which ends in mid-air, and from which a person may vanish, never to return. Indeed, a man might well have lost himself in the sapling and bramble brake at the end of our road. Bert Westmacott was not at that time working regularly at Shallows, but now he came back for a while. He viewed the wilderness with pleasure, and went off to collect bill-hook and axe. Within a day or two the usual spiral of smoke proclaimed the outward creeping fringe of civilization. After ten days the plot was cleared, and all that reminded us of former savagery was a big pile of bean-poles and several mounds of pale grey ash. Yet the floor of the clearing, smooth and green from a distance, was a deception, for it was studded with the close-cut butts of the saplings and the long, tenacious bramble roots. Below everything bracken roots were woven into a buried mat which extended the length and breadth of the garden. Nevertheless, we decided, some moorland tractor owner used to the outrageous upland applications of machinery, would surely plough for us.

I was wary of a candidate who was separated from me by the length of a telephone wire, and sought one within visiting distance. Thus, I hoped, I would be able to call on him during sickness and learned by local gossip if he was verily on holiday, or his machine dismantled. I was, therefore, pleased when Harry George Pengelly's young relative, Athelstan, agreed to come along in a few days and rip th' old patch all up for me.

I let the first two arranged dates slip by with no more than a reproach, but when the third passed I set off to find Athelstan. Drummond, the new tenant of Westhill, was near his drive gate, standing in contemplation of a tangled shrubbery. He had discarded the ulster to disclose a jacket which had once been of Donegal tweed. A purist might argue that it still was Donegal, despite the large areas replaced by leather patches, but if so its general mien was so despondent that I felt it could only have been born during the Trouble.

I passed the time of day, and, to make sure that the mercurial

Athelstan had not recently gone up the lane, inquired whether Drummond had seen him. I did not at that time know that Drummond, who did not often go from home, heard of every movement in the countryside. He was able to tell me that Athelstan and his tractor were temporarily out of commission, owing to a singular concatenation of circumstances.

It appeared that Athelstan had for several days been dragging timber from a wood above his farm, to which the approach was by a field so steep that the ground swelled up towards the vertical. At dusk Athelstan had found himself unusually thirsty and bethought himself of one of the inns at Rattleford. For one reason and another it was not at the time domestically expedient to go back to his farm and collect his car. He determined, therefore, to make a wide detour behind the wood, circle the farm out of earshot, and thus attain his goal without worry to anyone.

The manœuvre was successful, and after a quenching in pleasant company, Athelstan undertook the return journey with one or two companions, who were desirous of fresh air, standing on the back axle. A vein of cunning worthy of a Borgia prompted Athelstan to approach his home by the route from which he would have been expected had he returned direct from his work. To attain the wood across country with but a crescent moon to lend shadows to the rocks and holes was as sporting an achievement as to finish the course of the Midnight Steeplechase. The fearless crew had every reason to be proud of themselves as at last they and their iron steed stood poised for that last leap in the dark—the descent of the near-vertical field.

What happened no man will ever know, but now that Drummond recounted the tale I remembered the night in question. I remembered how Tessa and I, taking a bedtime turn among the trees, had heard the clatter of Athelstan's Fordson away towards the southern skyline. We had remarked on a devotion to work which must have been unique in all Devon, and listened as the clatter swelled to a roar and mounted to a crescendo which was cut as suddenly as when a hand throttles a screaming woman.

That moment when uproar was swamped by silence must have been the commencement of the great roll, when the tractor and riders rolled and somersaulted from wood to lane, like so many spillikins. No great harm resulted to the expedition beyond bruises and sprains and their mechanical equivalents, but I could see that trouble would follow for our hopes of a garden.

I went to see Athelstan, uncertain whether to offer condolences because of disaster, or congratulations on an outstanding feat of daring. He was, I thought, quite sorry to be robbed of the chance to show his mental agility in the forming of excuses for not carrying out his ploughing contract. There was no call for any as long as the Fordson leant against a wall in the yard, looking like a memento of a battlefield.

In the following weeks I went through the familiar routine of making arrangements, sending reminders, and drifting away to the next hope. We had the frosts of February and March, which would have done much for the upturned furrows; we had the April rains and the gentle steaming of the ground under the waxing sun; and we came to May.

Tessa now made the suggestion that we make known our needs to some of the displaced admirals, generals, counsellors, and the like, who had sought asylum about Rattleford from the post-War economic storm. At the first attempt we hooked a naval man who had burgeoned into a Ferguson owner. Of course he would be delighted to come; at the same time his wife would collect some azalea suckers which we had severed from their parents and set aside for her.

The sailor arrived on his Ferguson promptly to the minute. He wore a torn check shirt, a hat in which he obviously cleaned out the hen-house, and oily shorts held up with an Old Etonian tie. Repute had it that he was one of the wealthiest of the newcomers; certainly he usually dressed the part of a man who was not concerned about his credit. His wife turned up in a shooting-brake as I was directing the sailor up the bridle-path. She wore a commando beret, a seaman's jersey, baggy breeches not unlike an eastern female's pantaloons, rough farm-lad's stockings, and army boots. An extremely valuable pearl necklace hung like a halter over the jersey. She took a spade from the back of the brake and went off to find Tessa and the azalea suckers.

I

The sailor tackled the patch in the wood with the insouciance traditionally shown by a naval landing-party when set against great odds. The job was more properly one for a powerful caterpillar tractor. The roots of the young saplings which we had cut down checked the plough; the meandering and tenacious bramble roots wrapped themselves about the coulter and draw-bar; but worse than either were the bracken roots. They formed an interwoven brown mat, whose thickness was the full depth of the furrow, and whose area was as big as our garden. Over and above the panting of the tractor and the heaving and straining of the plough, we heard all the while the tearing of the bracken roots; the sound was like that of a piece of calico being ripped very slowly for an infinitely long time.

In the end we finished the ploughing. We harrowed, and after a few hot days Tessa and I raked the surface debris and burned it in many heaps about the third of an acre whose rich humus gave promise of a good first crop of potatoes, which are very partial to a mulching of dead and crumbled bracken. Ours would have many decades worth to nourish them. The sailor came again with his ridge plough, and our crop at last was in.

We took many a walk up the new path that spring and early summer to look at the sprouting of our potatoes. Almost, I think, we were able to spot each new head of earth-encrusted leaves as the haulms came through to daylight. This, we felt, was the highest endeavour of our species—to turn waste ground to productive plot.

CHAPTER TEN

*Hens and the spring celebration—Byron—The pig-slaughtering
—Juno the corgi—Louise's animal friends—The rabbits*

THROUGHOUT our time at Shallows we were not concerned
always with the vegetable-life which faced us as every turn,
climbed negligently over the house, and speedily came in through
any window which was left open for a few days. As always, a profusion of plant-life encouraged a variety of animal species.

Domestically we had, of course, the she-cat Pandy, who might
fairly have been described as a kitten factory; the hens; a pig from
time to time; and a corgi who joined us at one of Louise's birthdays.

The hens, although considered unlovable birds by Tessa and I,
did their share towards the children's education. In the early days
they had taught something of the egg and its fertilization; in other
words, that it takes two to make a world and that posterity is ovoid.
They taught also the evolution of superstition, and showed how
Christian religious teaching had been wise enough not to destroy the
old high-days, but to move in upon them. Easter was the particular
lesson taught by Primrose and her successors, and it was illustrated
with all the symbolism of coloured eggs, well hidden.

The Christians were fortunate to find that the egg was one of the
properties of the ancient spring festival, for it needed but a slight re-
emphasis on values to declare it the symbol not merely of life, but
resurrection. A thousand years before Jesus' blood was spilt the
Chinese dyed their spring eggs crimson to signify the colour of life.

The spring celebration has been common to most lands of the
northern hemisphere since man developed enough brain to learn
superstition. The Anglo-Saxon countries honoured Easter, sometimes called Eoster, the Spring Goddess, and April, so typically her
month, was known as Eoster-monach. It was naturally enough
one of the most joyful occasions of the year, when the mists and

bitter frosts of northern winter melted before a resurrected sun and the Earth Goddess, the Mother, showed promise of a fruitfulness soon to be born: greenness, growth, and food.

It was easy to add to this tradition the new Christian reason for a rejoicing which fell, by good fortune, at this very time. The egg, so long reverenced as the mystical seed of life by primitive peoples, eventually received Papal blessing. Pope Paul V made use of its prominence, and took it into the Church with this prayer:

"Bless, O Lord, we beseech Thee, this Thy creature of eggs, that it may become a wholesome sustenance to Thy faithful servants, eating in thankfulness to Thee, on account of the Resurrection."

Thus the Resurrection of Jesus mingled with the resurrection of the year.

Our egg-dyeing at Shallows was a big undertaking, for the children would expect to discover three or four nests on an Easter morning, and demanded a variety of colour. We used an old recipe to achieve bright yellow, by boiling eggs together with onion skins; cochineal in various strengths gave a range from pink to red; but for greens and blues we relied on household dyes, long salved in little bottles by Tessa from some earlier garment transformation.

In more leisured days eggs used to be written upon, or sometimes engraved. If you write on the shell with a wax pencil before boiling in the dye the egg will eventually come out with white inscriptions and designs on its coloured ground.

The engraving used to be done with a steel point, which inscribed by removing the dye. The work was at one time raised to the status of Art, and was done with exquisitely delicate scrolling.

A favourite design was the Easter hare. The hare, that uncanny spirit, was sacred to Mother Eastre and other vernal goddesses, and itself was credited with laying the kaleidoscopic eggs in the tussocks of grass where it had made its form.

Our Easters at Shallows have thus always been exciting, for the vibrations of the primitive life which had thickly crowded the Moor still influence those who live upon it.

The children discovered an affection for the one pig which we reared which exceeded that shown to the hens. A pig is, of course, a lovable animal whose sense of fun especially endears it to the

young. This particular pig, Byron, did not live in the place prepared in the top linhay, but with a pig of Bert Westmacott's which
occupied a hut in the corner of Bert's chicken field. One reason
for this choice of domicile was that Bert was able to feed two pigs
with one bucket, so to speak; but the more important reason was
that Tessa insisted that Byron must have company.

The children grew very fond of the pig, and what with one thing
and another—such as my ignorance of the channels by which a
Ministry-signed death warrant might be obtained—Byron grew
to be a very big pig indeed. He might, I suppose, have gone on to
beat record after record, had Bert not said that 'twas like tending
an elephant to keep 'un fed proper.

In the end we got our licence to make away with Byron, and I
questioned Bert about the procedure on the day; about transport
to the slaughter house, for instance, and the appointment of an
executioner.

"You'm not for sending 'un off to abbatoir!" he exclaimed, much
concerned. "There isn't no manner of means of telling 'tis yourn
carcase as 'ee'll get back. Let be with me to fix 'un up."

But if Bert was concerned at my plan, I was more so at his when
he unfolded it a little later. He had discovered an ex-butcher relative of Harry George Pengelly who was living not far away in
retirement, and who still possessed a desirable licence to slaughter.
He was willing enough to officiate just for the hell of it, and a slab
of liver. He was, however, a little frail, and Herbert Rice therefore
was going to come along to help with the lifting, and would accept
the chitterlings as a fee.

The locale was to be the verge of the lane outside Bert's cottage.
This was a most convenient spot, for just beyond the cottage was a
little shed in which Byron might spend his last night in meditation,
and have no more than a few steps to take in the morning. Furthermore, the open spout from which the cottage got its water gushed
through the hedge just there; while over the low garden wall Bert
had long ago constructed an outdoor boiler which would supply
the hot water for scalding off the bristles. It was then proposed to
lay Byron on a stretcher—borrowed from Harry George—and
carry him through Mrs Westmacott's kitchen to the scullery. This

had a beam in the roof which Bert would shore up, and over which he would throw the end of the rope from which Byron was to dangle ready to be cut up. Mrs Westmacott would, for her trouble, be very happy to have Byron's head to make brawn. This last request was Biblical, and I briefly pictured Mrs Westmacott soliciting her gift with the heavily seductive dancing of a Dartmoor Salome.

I was most alarmed by the proposed plan, whose various provisions, I felt sure, bristled with penalties should the authorities learn of it.

"Bah!" cried Bert. "'Tisn't likely any of they old inspectors'll come out along of we this time of year. 'Tis summer they do come, a-picnicing and a-frolicing with they young typist maids."

As an afterthought Bert warned me that I too would be required to lend a hand.

"Un'll be mortal heavy to lift up on beam," he pointed out.

Thus it seemed that, as well as risking a fine and imprisonment for flouting regulations, I was also to assist at the shambles.

The children were not badly put out when they learned that Byron was to be translated to a sphere of greater usefulness. They were just as prepared to eat him as they had been the hens, and, since they were really very fond of him, would no doubt vie with one another in lauding his flavour. It was, however, felt that they would be better out of the way at the moment of translation, and we arranged for them to take a rucksack full of food to a point on the moor which would be beyond the range of Byron's upper register of vocal attainment.

On the day I found a busy scene outside Bert's cottage. Over the wall Bert was stoking under his cauldron with ritualistic fervour. Herbert Rice was trying the stretcher here and there to ensure freedom from wobble; it was a simple contrivance, comprising ladderlike rungs dowelled into the thick poles which did for handles, and the whole standing on four short legs. Hung on the hedge was the basket for the chitterlings—a big one like those used by baker's roundsmen, with a spotless white cloth folded in the bottom. Harry George Pengelly's relative was laying out his weapons on a canvas hold-all spread on a boulder.

Herbert Rice went into the shed to lasso the principal actor, who came out like an express engine from a tunnel. We fell upon Byron, whose streamlined shape gave no hold save ears and tail, and with difficulty arrested his progress and directed him towards the stretcher, on to which with stupendous effort we raised him, one end at a time.

Our lane was not frequented by much traffic at this time of year, but no sooner was Byron laid like a sacrifice upon his rude altar, and Harry George Pengelly's relative, like a High Priest, was bent over him knife in hand, than the first car load of acquaintances drove by. They slowed a moment, fascinated by the macabre scene; then accelerated away under pressure from a lady passenger who had, I knew, always considered the Shallows family rather wild, and would now be able to tell her dearest friends that we were not wild, but savage. And so it went throughout the bloody rites. The passage of friends would not have disturbed me, for any one of them might have been involved in such an affair, but for the grace of God. It was from the passing of my acquaintances that I wished in vain to be spared.

At last the moor was solaced by its usual quiet. Bert handed buckets of scalding water across the wall, with which Herbert Rice sluiced the shell which had so recently entertained the personality of Byron. Following the scalding, Harry George Pengelly's relative scraped away the bristles, until in the end the corpse was unseemly naked.

"Reckon likely un's fit now," said Bert at last, though a less fit pig I had never seen.

At that we took each a corner of the rude stretcher and bore the remains of Byron towards Bert's front door, moving so slowly because of the extreme weight that we might have been mistaken for respectful bearers at a funeral. We managed fairly well through the big kitchen, but came to a halt at the door which led to the scullery passage, because the stretcher was too wide to pass.

Byron looked mountainous now we had him confined within four walls, dwarfing his surroundings. We were at a loss beside his impassive bulk of some eighteen-score pounds until Mrs Westmacott, who had been watching gravely, squeezed past into the scullery, and returned pushing in front of her a mangle. The mangle was composite with a table, whose sturdy iron legs rolled on castors. This was, we though, a splendid piece of improvisation, and did Mrs Westmacott great credit.

It was not easy to transfer Byron from the stretcher to the table of the mangle which was about a foot higher. Also, the table was quite small, and even when Byron's middle section rested upon it we still had to take much of the weight of his protruding extremities. In the end Bert and Harry George's relative went in front, cradling Byron's head and fore-trotters, while Herbert Rice, in a crouching position, thrust his head between the hind legs and thus supported them on his shoulders. It was my duty to stand on the open side of the table, and keep Byron from slipping off sideways by thrusting him against the mangle rollers.

We went well through the inner door of the kitchen and along the passage, but the turning into the scullery was too sharp for us. Byron and the mangle stuck transversely across the end of the passage, trapping me in the corner and cutting off Herbert Rice from all of us. Bert and Harry George's relative were themselves just within the scullery threshold and were able to see the problem clearly. They decided after some discussion that the only hope of ever moving Byron from his present resting-place was to lift the forward end of the mangle round until it cleared the doorpost. To achieve this would, they considered, require all hands.

In the position where Byron now found himself he could not slip sideways off the table, since he was jammed partly against the passage wall and partly against the doorpost. Therefore I was free to go round to the head end if I could discover a feasible route. I asked Mrs Westmacott whether, provided I could return to the kitchen, I could get in through the scullery window by going round outside the house. This was apparently impossible, since the window was small, high up, not made to open, and barred. Bert then suggested that if I could work myself up until I lay on Byron he and Harry George's relative could drag me through the gap between the pig and the top of the doorway. This manœuvre we managed to accomplish by co-operation, and it only remained for Herbert Rice to join us.

Herbert, of course, was not free to leave his place between the hind legs, for Byron might even now slip off backward, and if he did we knew that we were done. It was now that Mrs Westmacott showed a staunch loyalty by offering to do substitute for Herbert, so that he might wriggle forward over Byron as I had done. The delicate task of changing places was accomplished with skill, and a minute or two later Herbert joined the rest of us in the scullery, and several good heaves in unison so positioned the mangle that it had a straight run into the room.

We still deemed it necessary to have a rear-guard, and were not satisfied that Mrs Westmacott could sustain that role when Byron was on the move. Herbert Rice, being small and quite nimble, volunteered therefore to make the return journey over Byron, and successfully accomplished it.

All that remained to do was to give a smooth, steady pull, and Byron lay at last with his hind legs under the beam from which he had all along been destined to hang. While Bert and I slung the rope over the beam, Harry George's relative inserted a stout stave through Byron's hind-leg sinews, and tied thereto one end of the rope. While he steadied Byron on the mangle table, the rest of us took the strain on the rope. Byron, however, showed in death the same obstinacy for which he had been well known in life, and, try as we would, we could raise little more than his hinder parts a few inches from the table. Obviously the pull over the beam was much too up-and-down and really called for a pulley. We made one more attempt, all swinging together on our end of the rope, but Byron would not go up. Instead, the beam gave a sudden groan, and one of Bert's shoring-poles slipped, striking Harry George's relative, who collapsed across Byron.

Mrs Westmacott had been admirably calm up to now, but the combination of the warning from the beam, the clatter of the falling pole, and the alarming sight of Harry George's relative lying athwart Byron was too much for her nerves. She fled back into the kitchen, crying that the pig would bring the house down about our ears, and that we had better look to our souls. However, when we had revived Harry George's relative with a little cold water, and had wedged back more firmly the fallen pole, she returned as far as the scullery doorway, though a little fearfully.

It was now clear that we should be unable to swing Byron up
by means of a straight pull over the beam. Accordingly, we decided that Herbert Rice, assisted by Harry George's relative, should
get his back under Byron's hind quarters, and that Bert and I, as
the two heaviest men, should win what rope we could as Herbert
lifted. This method worked better than we had dared hope, in
spite of the poor help from Harry George's relative, who was still
very shaky. Within two or three minutes all of Byron was in the
air, except for his head and chest which were still supported by the
table. Byron's rope-borne weight now counterbalanced that of
Bert and me, and we had to coax Mrs Westmacott to swing with us
on the rope while Herbert and Harry George's relative put forth the
last ounce of their strength.

Had Byron eaten as much as another potato at his last meal I do
not believe that we would have succeeded, so narrowly was our
combined strength balanced against his weight. But at last his
head and chest swung free of the mangle table, and the whole body
smacked Harry George's relative in the ribs, sending him flying
into the sink, which was as big as a horse-trough. Bert made the
free end of the rope fast to a stout hook in the wall, and Byron was
at last where we wanted him.

Harry George's relative opened Byron up—a little savagely, I
thought—and Herbert Rice filled his basket with chitterlings with
the eager lust of a revolutionary *tricoteuse*. The liver was now
shared out fairly all round, and Phase One of the operation was over.
Phase Two was arranged for mid-morning next day, when the
Rattleford butcher's roundsman, a powerful man and a skilled dis-
sector, was to dismember the body and deliver the pieces by van at
Shallows.

We all accepted a mug of strong tea from Mrs Westmacott,
and dispersed wearily to our homes, each bearing with us various
fleshly reminders of Byron.

Next morning, little later than first light, I was disturbed in my
sleep by movement in the kitchen, by laboured breathing, and
those heavy, unechoing thuds which one associates with deeds of
violence. I lay quiet for a while, to allow my subconscious to tell
my half-waking mind what was to happen in the house that morning,

but there was enough wakefulness in my brain for it to be over-clever, remembering that no one was expected at the house till the van came with the parts of Byron. The sounds which had come from the kitchen now posed a sinister question, and I could rest easy no longer, but must arise and see.

It was evident that the butcher's roundsman had altered the plan for Phase Two, and had delivered Byron at a very early hour, having, I suppose, done his grim work in Bert's scullery by candlelight, like a monster in a horror tale. At any rate, our kitchen was a charnel house. The table was heaped with bloody meat; with huge sides and flanks. Another mound rested on some spread sacks on the hearth. There were big tin baths filled with smaller and unidentifiable pieces.

Thus rudely disturbed from my bed, and now shocked by the gruesome transformation of our kitchen, and wondering how any-one was to cook breakfast, and, if they did, whether it would be eaten, I was turned cold by the sight of Byron's head looking out over the side of a basket set on the seat of the fireside arm-chair. As I later learned, Mrs Westmacott had considered that Bert had been forward in demanding the head as a perquisite, and had insisted that it be delivered to me so that I might present it to her with my own hands if I was willing, and not be confronted with a *fait accompli*.

Byron looked at me, unnerved as I was, with his usual expression of impishness, tinged with malice. I was glad that Mrs Westmacott was to have his brawn, which might well, I though, make the mischief of a poltergeist.

Phase Three, the curing, was under the direction of Mrs Westmacott, who spent her days with us during this trying period. My role was simply to clear out the larder so that the slate slabs might be used as mortuary shelves, and to fix strong hooks in the attic ceiling, where Byron was to hang. Tessa was making the muslin bags to protect him throughout his sojourn aloft.

The tumult and confusion came to an end eventually, for even chaos is finite, and Shallows became outwardly its peaceful self. Yet brooding over our heads was the great bulk of Byron, at once a challenge and a reproach to the avarice of appetite. We came to eat him as a duty in the determination to get Shallows to ourselves again. At the consumption of each rasher we felt that we had crawled fractionally closer to our distant goal.

Our corgi could not really be classed as a domestic animal, for she became one of us, showing just as much perversity, cantankerousness, sense of fun, and, for all I know, intelligence. She belonged really to Louise, and the two of them were inseparable within a few days of meeting. Her name, Juno, was not at all appropriate, for she was a very small corgi indeed, and would not have done well at the show bench because of lack of size. She was a black and tan. That is, her head, chest, and legs were fox-colour, strongly tinged with the shade of auburn which many a woman would give much to possess; her back was black, deeply glossy; and her belly and hind quarters very pale fawn. The bushiness of the fawn fur on her hind legs, set off by a waggling gait, reminded me of Turkish trousers worn by a self-confident top-girl in a harem.

Many years ago, when I had bought a farm in Wales, I had taken over with the sheep-dogs a working corgi, the traditional cattle-dog of Wales. Like the sheep-dog, the corgi has had to earn its living, and has developed the ready wit of the workers, together with an affinity with man not readily developed by breeds which have deteriorated in idleness. The corgi now has become a fashionable dog, a favourite at Crufts, and possessing a high social value. Yet for once the breeders have not spoilt it by artificial selection of points which are detrimental to both intelligence and physique. It has not suffered, and is now unlikely to suffer, the degradation of the airedale, for instance, or the wire-haired fox-terrier, both once allies of man, honest working dogs, but now canine caricatures in their show-bench versions.

Juno's pedigree was unwritten in its early pages, for her ancestors had come across Europe with the late Bronze Age Celts, minding their cattle for them, sleeping against the herdsmen in the glow of many a camp-fire during that half-nomad trek of the Brythons from the Danube to Britain. The Brythons and the corgis still live side by side in partnership in Wales, perhaps the oldest specific association of human and animal which has survived.

The half-grown bitch worried us at first, for although she settled

down quickly, put the cats and hens in their place, nipped tradesmen round the heels in lieu of cattle hooves, and established herself
as Louise's shadow, she appeared never to eat. Yet she grew in size
and weight, had inexhaustible energy, and showed health in the
shine of her coat. The fact that her bowl of food was always eventually emptied did not signify that Juno was replete, for the cats,
or stray fox-hounds brought in by the children, might well have
been the diners.

The truth was, of course, that Juno was a secret eater. She would
rarely so much as sniff at a meal even with the family only present;
she would not turn her head towards it were a stranger about. Yet
we began to realize that she kept an eye on the dish, menacing the
cats in a silent manner designed not to attract our notice: the sort of
tacit threat which parents grimace at a badly behaved child when in
polite company, a 'you wait till I get you by yourself' promise.

In the end she always ate the lot. I know several humans with
similar habits.

As the children became more and more venturesome Juno assumed
a fussier and fussier role of nursemaid. She barked when they
approached danger; growled at and nipped the heels of companions
of whom she did not approve; sat by the hour in rain or cold outside some house or cottage into which the children had wandered;
and bore with the resignation of a tormented early Christian all
the humiliation of wearing doll's pants and a sun-bonnet.

Tessa and I came to benefit from Juno's devotion to the children,
which was paramount over her secondary duty to us, for our minds
were much eased during their long absences, knowing that the dog
was with them on tor, in bog and stream and wood. It was not very
long before Juno was so much one of us that our family became five,
and because of the closeness of our relationship with her she came to
know our very thoughts by a divination as exact as Yogi telepathy.
Only sometimes were we sorry of Juno's close approach to our
mental ways, for there were times when she tried to talk to one or
other of us, making the strangled vocal noises of a dumb human,
desisting when she saw that she must fail, and creeping away in
misery. But Juno never remained miserable for long, and after
one of these bouts she would come back among us, look up, draw

back her lips to show a delightful smile, and presently would open
her mouth in whole-hearted laughter at the efforts to form the
words which were so unnecessary between her and us.

The children, of course, wanted her to have puppies. But Juno
was like a nanny who had vowed to remain devoted to her charges.
We found after a year or two that there was no need to keep her
guarded at her mating season. Though the dogs from the four
corners of the parish prowled as restlessly as the hosts of Midian,
yet Juno would have none of them, showing so startling a ferocity
at any near advances that many a Rattleford masher bears her scars
to this day.

There was a time, however, when tragedy was to come to Juno's
life. We were at the time away from home, and decided that now
we were within reach of several good corgi kennels we would
persuade Juno that she had our blessing on her union, and that the
children were old enough to spare her attentions for a while.

She did, it is true, show more interest in the corgi stud dog of
one of the kennels than ever she had in the most swashbuckling of
our local Rattleford riff-raff, yet even he made the one advance too
many, and was bitten.

It was two or three days later that Louise came in to tell us that
Juno had fallen in love. She had, it seemed, cast her eyes upon a
handsome young red corgi dog who sometimes passed up the pavement of the street in which we were then staying. Indeed, it became
noticeable that Juno let the cats eat the food which she would herself normally have secretly consumed. Her smile was gone. Hour
by hour she sat by the gate of the small town garden. In the end
we tracked down the owner of the red corgi, who was willing enough
to have his dog earn a stud fee.

Almost I was ashamed of Juno, who threw herself at the strange
dog's head like a spinster rendered uninhibited by drink, who is
going to toss her bonnet over the windmill if she dies for it. Perhaps
her ardour frightened the young dog; certainly he was, as his owner
warned us, as inexperienced as Juno. For nearly a week we had the
unhappiness of watching an unrequited love affair; of seeing Juno
run the gamut of excitement, eagerness, disillusionment, and despair. I do not think she will ever love one of her own kind again;

certainly her great capacity for affection is lavished now in an even more spendthrift way upon the children.

As Louise grew older we noticed that she showed a great interest in the wild life about the garden of Shallows, as well as in our domestic animals. But it was some time before we began to realize that the wild life reciprocated the interest.

Birds, of course, were always on the wing in the house, or twittering and dipping on a beam or a pelmet, and many of these Louise would catch. They must, I think, have been half willing; at any rate, once in her hand they crouched with an acquiesence only faintly tinged with apprehension.

Once I came upon her strolling in a not unusual day-dream, a toad squatting on her shoulder. He was a repulsive, warty beast, but seemed fond enough of the child. Louise had apparently known him for quite a while, and had often played with him at his home under a specific log in the linhay where we built up our firewood stocks. When winter came that year she tied a length of red wool to his hind leg so as to be able to know that he was still drowsing in his annual sleep under the log. While I had to see that that part of the pile remained undisturbed.

Louise's friendships in the animal kingdom were not always fortunate. I was walking one day down the lane with both the children when Mark Collins' Aberdeen Angus bull came rocking down towards us, his great head mowing between his knees, and his flanks brushing the fox-gloves on either side.

This, I thought, is when my friends will pity me and my enemies forgive. This may become one humble example to be held up as the justification of fatherhood. I whispered urgently to the children to make no sudden move, but gently to fade backward, and to climb over the gate not far behind us. As I had feared they both voiced noisy questions, peering past me.

"Oh!" cried Louise, running forward to pat the monster, "it's dear old Angus."

Her oddest pet was brought to her by the cat Pandy, whose current crop of kittens were at that time about a month old. Evidently Pandy had thought it time to develop their hunting instinct, for one bright August morning she brought in to them alive and unharmed what we thought at first was a mouse. It was Louise who saw the creature presented to the kittens, and was in time to snatch it away. She cradled it in her hands and showed it to Tessa, who recoiled. It was a bat; a pipistrelle, according to Louise. She told us that it was a variety which was readily tamed, and that it had already nipped her fingers, which was an excellent sign, being a token of affection.

It was an attractive little creature, clumsy when laid in the hand, but sleek in its tiny body, which was no bigger than a shrew-mouse's, and with a most intelligent, bright-eyed face. When we had all admired the bat, whom Louise named Whiskers after its facial adornment, which was worthy of a Dumas musketeer, the child wandered off with her new companion.

Louise sat down to lunch without remark, and it was only after a few minutes that Tessa noticed Whiskers, who was hanging upside down from Louise's lapel. Tessa might, perhaps, have put up with a skeleton at the feast, but she drew the line at a bat, even a very small one. Louise was indignant at what she fancied to be a slight upon Whiskers and, as she often did when in a resentful frame of mind, went off to sit with a book in a corner of the veranda. I came upon her there later on. She was reading Tennyson, who was then her favourite poet, and Whiskers, in his usual inverted position, was clinging to the top rail of her deck-chair.

I only saw them together once more that day. Louise was walking across the grass, and Whiskers was flitting about her head. It could have been no other bat in that brilliant August sunshine.

It happened that we went away for two or three weeks the very next morning, and Tessa and I thought that the incident of the bat was surely closed, for Whiskers was certainly not with us during our time from home.

It was the next spring that Tessa decided to give a special cleaning to the children's day nursery, which was that room with a veranda door which I had always coveted. Louise hovered about like an uneasy spirit.

The room had a typical Shallows ceiling following the pitch of the roof, which left a sort of inverted eave where the slope of the ceiling met the inner wall. There was here a recess which ran the length of the room, and which was a natural dust-trap. Louise watched with growing agitation as Tessa's ruthless brush began to scour one end of the ledge, and at last the child begged to be allowed to help. She pushed up a chair, and standing on it made some ineffective and furtive motions with a duster.

Tessa's suspicions, sharpened by experience, were quickly roused, and she peered into Louise's end of the crevice. She did not know what she might expect to see, except that it would undoubtedly be something forbidden—a hoard of mouldering food, or the corpse of some old friend such as the toad, preserved in an air-tight jar. She was certainly not prepared to encounter a pipistrelle bat in its usual up-side-down attitude, torpid, but in good health.

However, we had learned by now that we only shared our house with the other denizens of the garden. Not only birds and bats moved in upon us at will, but a mole recurrently appeared in the bathroom, and a vole no bigger than my thumb-nail in our bedroom.

The bats, in fact—cousins of Whiskers, I suppose—lived in some cavity of the barn-like sitting-room roof. Their access was through a knot-hole in the wood of the south gable, and at that precise nightly moment when twilight is about to be overwhelmed by darkness the first bat would launch himself into the air. The last night on which I counted, forty-one bats vacated our roof within ten minutes.

The bat is an illustration of the fate of a species which has taken the wrong turning in the devious maze of evolutionary trends. Many such species have died the death, and at this moment in time, during this present few thousand years, it is probable that the bat is a-dying.

We revile the bat as a haunter of eerie dwellings, as a fly-by-night, as a jackal who flits beside death's shadow. Yet it but hides by day from its enemies, and hunts in the minutes of twilight, and is likely to be found in churchyards, because there it finds peace.

The fact is that the bat should have man's sympathy, for man has been fortunate in his evolution to the position of dominant mammal, while his distant cousin, the little flying mammal of the dusk, has

K

not been fortunate. The air was no place for mammals, yet the bats have shown exemplary persistence and determination in following a dead-end road along which they have travelled too far to return.

Even now, after this long and lone divergence from the earthbound mammals, it seems to me that bats are more akin to man than many of his nearer companions. Charles Derennes, that acute French observer and friend of the bat, is convinced that the little creatures have a language; he even spells phonetically some of their expressions and gives the meaning. Certainly Louise's Whiskers had plenty of variety in his twittering, and the expression was understandable, even if we were too ignorant to translate the words.

Bats are not unlike us in some of our better habits, but do not, I believe, imitate our failings. For instance, they seem to mate for life, and they show the utmost affection for and devotion to their minute young, which are mostly born only children, less commonly as twins. In fact the birthrate probably just fails to balance the deathrate of the pitiable misfit species.

For the bat, existence is precarious and barely worth the struggle. It cannot see well in bright light, nor in darkness—at least, not well enough to hunt the minute aerial prey which itself is most plentiful at dusk. There is but that brief lowering hour when the little mammal, supported so laboriously on its crude wings, can find its food; and even during this short and vital period it must rest as frequently as must a man in the unfamiliar element of water, or in the thin atmosphere of unusual altitude.

In many a summer season this piteous outcast of nature can but maintain its daily strength, coming to winter and the long sleep of hibernation with no reserve of well-being. Shrouded in its silken wings, it yields to cold and time, and dies.

One year the children desired rabbits, and spent much time preparing a hutch and wired run in the belief that the rabbits would thus be induced to materialize. So they did, two chinchillas. I suppose we should have realized that hutch and run were but tokens, for within a week the chinchillas lived in the house, except for excursions among the vegetables.

It was curious that Pandy, who occasionally killed wild rabbits, the more often when she was rearing kittens, ignored the chinchillas even when they were sprawled in her own place on the kitchen hearth-rug. Indeed, the rabbits took on all the aggressiveness of the weak, for if a playful kitten investigated them with a tentative paw they would thump it in the ribs with their powerful hind legs, doing their best to kick it a mile in exchange for the inch it had taken.

In the garden the rabbits proved very trying to Tessa and me. They were less interested in vegetables than in flowers. The former we could guard with wire netting in their patches between the shrubs, but we did wish the flowers to grow uninhibited. We only had the two formal beds: those which formed two crescents about the foot of the big rhododendron clumps. It was on the growth of these that the chinchillas relentlessly fed. They showed strong preference for polyanthus and lupins—which was really quite thoughtful of them, for we had these in plenty, but were short of chrysanthemums, dahlias, and delphiniums.

At last we determined that the rabbits must be confined during the growing season in order to allow the edible parts of the plants to climb beyond their reach.

We passed the rabbits to some neighbouring children to look after during an absence from home. I suppose that their temporary guardians were unaware how deeply the seed of liberty was planted in those fur-coated breasts. At any rate, on our return we learned that the chinchillas had made a break for it, and had avoided recapture.

It was Louise, many weeks later, who saw the flash of grey in the wood. Sure enough, the rabbits had come home, and by chance or superior education were avoiding the mortal dangers which counterbalance the advantages of freedom. They had gained much in agility, and no longer could we eventually run them to earth, as in the days of sport on the herbaceous border.

Their influence has spread far and wide, and we have seen rabbits with the aristocratic dove-grey tint as far away as Kestor Rock itself.

CHAPTER ELEVEN

The fish-pond—Attacking the sluice—Visit from Hamish Drum-
mond—Venture into the wood—Clearing the pond—Pond-life
and a lesson in evolution—Sludge misused—The new sluice—
The pool is filled

IT seemed always to be in winter that we undertook summer
work at Shallows. We had built the causeway through the bog
during a spell of snow and sleet. Perhaps the hard fibres of our
northern being reacted vigorously to the challenge of foul weather.
At any rate, it was February when some instinct led Tessa to prod
the mud of the fish-pond with a bamboo.

The fish-pond lay in the bottom left-hand corner of the garden
as one looked up towards the wood and the moor beyond. The
angle in which it lay was formed by the junction of lane and bridle-
path.

It was a very stormy day when Tessa first prodded the pond with
her bamboo, so that when I heard her wild cries I ran out into the
rain, fearing that she was in difficulties in the weed-grown water.

Her excitement, however, was because her probing seemed to
indicate that beneath the mud was a bottom so hard that she wondered if it were concrete. I too secured a pole, and sounded all
round the sides and as far in towards the middle as I dared lean,
and everywhere my pole struck firm bottom.

We had always meant to clean out the pond some day, for year
by year the stream which fed it carried down its deposit of gravel
and mud; and each autumn the trees round the banks had shed their
leaves into the water, until Luke Fox's men had felled them for me.
But we had not hurried to tackle a task which promised little but
hard work, since we had expected to find no more than mud beneath mud and saw no hope of swimming.

It was now imperative to discover what made this hard bottom, and whether it extended over the whole floor of the pond. It was plain that we could only discover the truth by draining off the water so that I could wade to the central mud and there probe. There was a sluice in the bank of the pond, next to the lane, which opened into a deep-cut flow-away through the bank and dived under the earth and stone rampart which separated our garden from the lane, and which was topped by a row of sycamore-trees.

I had once or twice before had a go at the sluice, which was a wooden gate designed to slide in grooved side-posts. Unfortunately, the wood had swollen, and the gate was so firmly gripped that hitherto I had been unable to lift it. I now proposed to waste no time upon niceties and sprang into the flow-away ditch, axe in hand. It was a circumscribed position for axe-work, and I could do no more than peck at the wood, which was as hard as if petrified. Quite early in the operation I split the gate at a point about three feet below water-level and worked thereafter under a jet of high-pressure iced water, such as prison warders employ to subdue rioting convicted felons. In spite of being already wet through in the steady downpour, the added moisture was uncomfortable, being much colder than the rain. Tessa, however, egged me on as a Germanic matron would have urged her wounded spouse to rejoin battle with the Roman legionaries.

It was in a dusk prematurely born under lowering clouds that the sluice gave way. It came in towards me very suddenly and with the force of a charging war-horse, sweeping me back along my head-high ditch in a welter of splintered wood, weeds, and foam. I picked myself out of the farther end of the flow-away, and joined Tessa on the brink of the pond. The water-level fell rapidly through the considerable breach, in spite of a surface area of about eighty feet by forty; nevertheless it was quite dark before I was able to slide down the vertical bank. At the point where I found myself the mud did not come above my rubber boots, but was of a highly glutinous quality, immobilizing me at once. Tessa handed me a stout pole, and with this as a third leg I decided that I might be able to move towards the centre. Caution, however, prompted me to send Tessa for a light, and she returned presently with an old-fashioned candle-lantern.

It was when I had reached the very centre, and was crying above the wind the glad news that somewhere beneath the mud was rock-hard bottom, that I saw dimly that a figure had joined Tessa. The newcomer was strangely sinister in shadowy outline, and I did not guess that it was Hamish Drummond until I was near enough to recognize the ulster.

It appeared that he had been brought from a comfortable fireside by the rushing sound of mighty waters, and had been in time to watch a portion of his drive swept away by the unbridled licence of the contents of the pond released by my axe. Thereafter he had been an interested spectator of my peregrinations by lantern-light through the mud. He was too polite to say so in as many words, but it was clear to both of us that he considered us, at the least, eccentric. However, he trusted himself alone with us in the house when I decided that a hot rum would perhaps chase my blood through veins so constricted with cold that they could at the moment allow but a trickle to circulate.

Hamish Drummond obviously had the feeling that he was an intruder on our privacy, and that his dripping ulster might harm the carpet of our sitting-room. He stood, therefore, just within the door, and watched while I kicked off my boots by the fire and squatted a moment to warm while the rum took effect.

Talking of pools, he related the phenomenon of the appearance of eels within a few weeks of the construction of ponds on farms in the Canadian Prairie Provinces, and thence passed quickly over the mysterious transatlantic migrations of elvets, no more than a few millimetres in length. Shifting his stance, and accepting another rum, but declining to remove his wet ulster, Hamish recounted the qualities of swimming-pools which he had known in many parts of the world—with a digression, in Haiti, to visit some zombies—and, following this appraisal, gave us a brief costing for our own pond for (*a*) a concrete bottom and (*b*) walls in either brick, concrete, or tiles.

The children had listened with much fascination to this encyclopædic verbal doodling, and went unwillingly to bed. Hamish refused to share food with us, but leaned against the door-post to watch us devour scrambled eggs by the fire-light. He stood upright to drink his coffee with us, and remained thus until after midnight, when he remarked that his wife had a pie for him and he must say good-night.

The weather continued inclement, but neither Tessa nor I could leave the pond alone, and as a result every rough garment we possessed became saturated, and later scorched through impatient drying. The mud remained glutinous, despite the breach at the sluice, for not only rain fed it, but the flood-water of the stream next to the bridle-path. The stream was, in reality, a split from our main water-course. The split occurred somewhere in the top corner of the wood under cover of the thickest example of our jungles. Three fallen trees were here, lying one across the others; through them had grown willow and alder in those typical thick groups of shoots, each cluster of which thrust up stiffly like bristles in a yard broom. The bramble lacing was here especially thick and strong.

It had always been Tessa's wish, her ultimate goal, to be able to stroll up the bank of our main stream in shoes. The stream was a gem of its kind, made up of pools as quiet as the lustre of pearls, linked by diamond rapids. As the tilt of the wood lifted to the moor, there were miniature gorges and waterfalls, funnelled through arching walls of evergreen. There were in spring thick carpets of the pale, lilac-coloured bog violet, the blooms half as big as pansies, and dense drifts of wild hyacinths, blue and white. The rocks were rich with lichen and Devon fern.

These delights we had glimpsed, but never enjoyed.

Now, forced by conditions in the fish-pond to reach the point where the streams diverged, I began the ascent of the bank of the main branch, assisted by The Machine. We crossed the causeway, whose building had been an essential if The Machine were to enter the wood, and followed the kitchen-garden route for fifty yards up the stream bank. The route then continued diagonally across the heart of the wood, and The Machine and I remained poised, before tearing our way up the bank, which was from here on unknown.

We did tear our way, as much as cut it, for the brambles wound themselves about the axle of The Machine, about its engine and handles, and about its operator. The roots of these tentacles were usually far beyond the reach of our cutter-bar, and, indeed, many of them were rooted across the stream, and had slid across on fallen boughs like snakes; or dropped from living ones, like panthers. Even so, The Machine fought the jungle like an infant Hercules, and with the same blend of brute force and bloody ignorance previously displayed by that prototype of Buck Ryan, save that it was I who was bloody in this modern labour.

We carved our way for quite a distance before The Machine sank in a bog. I reminded myself that all this was really in aid of the fish-pond, denied myself the pleasure of draining the bog, lugged The Machine on to firm ground, and proceeded thence, bent double, following the bed of the stream to the place where it forked. I felt as pleased at reaching this untrodden spot as if I were the first man to squat beside the source of the White Nile. And, beneath overreaching branches twined with brambles, squat I had to, while I dammed off the entry to the fish-pond stream.

I left the jungle quite reluctantly to return to the mud of the pond, which an examination showed was bound together by the roots of a plant which grew individually like a giant dock, but in close community with similar plants. This water-growth came up reluctantly, being rooted in the liquefaction below, which clung to it as if it had the knowledge that without the unifying properties of the roots the mud would ooze away through the sluice gap. It finally rendered up each forkful of the sturdy waterweed with a sullen plop, which was near enough to a groan. The forkful was always very heavy, for the plants were not divisible, and one had to take them complete, sodden, and with a bucketful of mud clinging to the roots. When the load was poised for throwing, one of three annoyances overtook one: on the draw-back of the fork before the outward thrust a proportion of the mud dropped into one's knee-boots; or, the power of the outward thrust being nullified by the tenacity of the plant, the load slid back into the mud a foot or two distant; or the load would not leave the fork at all.

This last situation, difficult in itself, became disastrous when combined with immobilization of the legs. Naturally, when holding extended a half-hundredweight of bound mud on the end of a fork, one could only retain balance by a lightning shuffle of the feet. If this facility of equipoise were denied the load returned to its native ooze, taking the foiled thrower with it. Of course, the whole affair took place in a flash, and to the onlooker the action seemed a deliberate dive. More than once I noticed Hamish Drummond's cap looking at me from above the shelter of the ulster as he passed along the lane, but he forbore to call any comment, and on each occasion disappeared up Westhill drive in an aura of lifted eyebrows.

Gradually the weeds and their attendant mud-pats were thrown up on the banks, where later I used them to fill in holes and hollows in the surround; and gradually the remaining ooze, constantly disturbed by my staggerings and plungings, and thus kept in suspension in the water, was carried through the sluice breach. When all was done it was Tessa who identified the weed. It was water plantain, and, according to the catalogue which had enlightened her, was worth three shillings and sixpence a root. We calculated that our surround had been levelled with fifty sovereigns' worth. However, I consoled Tessa with a little cynicism, for it was already our experience that the retail price of a nurseryman's list bore no relation to the price he would pay a supplying grower, nor, for that matter, would the public pay much to the amateur grower, feeling, we supposed, that he would only have burned the stuff if he had not been lucky enough to find a customer, and ought therefore to be more than content with a token payment.

I penetrated the top jungle again and turned in the stream full strength to help flush away the remaining ooze which lingered in the pond. For a couple of days Tessa and I and both children waded to and fro, swooshing and swishing with home-designed implements, and watching the out-flow change through various shades of coffee, from *noir* to *café au lait*, and thence to the pale grey of British Railways buffet beverage.

At last the bottom of the pool showed clear, and was revealed as a hard blue-white clay, not unlike that associated with the rotted granite in which china clay is found. It was so hard that a pickaxe could only flake up irregular pieces as big as bits of coke. The clay was lightly covered with fine yellow gravel. We were all delighted at discovering this foundation, which even had an advantage over concrete in that it would never become slimy.

The whole floor of the pool was now covered with an inch or two of water, which never drained quite away, and here and there were a few shallow depressions where the depth was greater, and which were kept fresh by the inflow from the stream. It was now that the water had clarified that we saw trout in the pools, and a couple of eels. We saw the eels jack-knifing their way across the shallows. One was a thick fellow about eighteen inches long, with a frill of fin along his back, and the other was not much smaller. I shouted for a bucket, hoping to catch them and take time to decide what to do with them, for I wanted to discourage them from using the pool any more. But by the time the children had quarrelled about who should carry the pail, and had jointly fallen down the bank with it, both eels had slipped through the inlet and into the stream, and had vanished with a sinuous gesture apiece which was derisory. It was only when they were gone that I realized that I held a shovel and might readily have slain them, not only as the ultimate discouragement, but for food.

I looked sheepishly at Tessa, but it had not occurred to her either that we might have exercised the human right to kill. In any case, excitement had now developed in one of the little pools, in which a rainbow trout was floundering desperately. It was a very nice fish, weighing about three quarters of a pound. The bucket was at hand now, and I scooped the fish up and passed it to Tessa on the bank, who tipped it into the leat by which our main stream was conducted under the lane and through Westhill shrubbery to the pool before that house's front door.

It was a few days later that Hamish remarked to us that a new trout had taken up residence in his pond. Tessa demanded to see it, and, on being shown, affirmed that it was ours, and had only been tipped in the leat instead of the stream in a moment of such excitement that she was not to be held responsible for her actions, and that the gift was therefore null and void. Hamish gave us a few facts about the habits of trout, holding out good hopes that this particular fish would return to Shallows at spawning time, and as an example of artificial pisciculture quoted costs and statistics of rearing in a Hampshire hatchery. Meanwhile he offered to drain his pond and return the trout to Tessa, which reparation she hesitantly declined in expectation of its voluntary return next season.

This was not the only trout, though the biggest, which we deported from the bottom of the pond. In the end Tessa or the children caught a dozen or so, which they took care to place in the other stream, which did not give so ready a way of escape from our garden.

These floundering fish replayed before our eyes that earliest nativity play, depicting for us the first step of water-life towards animal existence and manhood. They showed us in mime what happened when the crowded, land-locked pools of the youthful world became fouled and stagnant; how a few fish would part the surface between their dead, belly-up companions, and would flop on to the ooze of the bank, searching with blind instinct for running water or a fresher pool; of the fraction who gained the mud but a smaller fraction would have survived that historic trek; and but a fraction of the survivors would have trekked yet again, and slowly bred into their young the tolerance of land which became the characteristic of the amphibians, in whom man's family tree is rooted. Hardship and the desperate will to live drove the fish into the unknown; had they not been driven so, man would not have become the heir of both their hope and their desperation. If in those distant days God and Michael had stepped across space to examine for a moment the new world and its life struggling to evolve, He might have asked Michael to transport the gasping fish to clean water in a bucket. But if Michael and his bucket had been there to spare the hardship and restrain the daring, then man would not have been born.

We look at the stars a lot at Shallows. The pointed fingers of the conifers indicate significantly the winking lights of the myriad other houses of creation; the other ponds whose water may be fresher; the gaps between us and them no more uncrossable than were those first few feet of ooze and rock. It is not so much man who is indomitable, but life. It is life in the physical embodiment of man, and of such creatures that, Noah-like, he may carry with him, that will flow at last across separating space to flourish anew in the *Lebensraum* of empty worlds or even to coalesce with the life which already pulses in them and maybe thinks.

Perhaps man will one day find his God. Yet the divinity may be unrecognizable, for it may not be that man is made in God's image, but that man, with his inherent conceit, has misconceived God to be in man's. But more isolated than the lot of some miscast astral pioneers, circling in endless orbit around some uncaring star, will be the lot of our species if we find that man is God and we are at last alone.

We did not waste all the sludge from the bottom of the pond just in levelling of holes and hollows, but spread some on flower-beds and vegetable plots. We had heard that the nurserymen along the valley of the Tamar grew their rich crops with the help of such fertilizer. Our sludge was made of rotted humus, which should have been a prime nourishing agent, yet we were disappointed. Indeed, so far was the mud from being beneficial that it killed a lot of seed-lings. It was Bert Westmacott, surprisingly, who told us our mistake, which was in using the mud fresh. The Tamar men let their dredgings lie in heaps for six months to aerate and sweeten.

Late spring was on us by the time the old fish-pond was cleaned, the banks tidied up, brambles rooted out, and the trees which had been felled by Luke Fox trimmed off, split with wedges, and removed. The children were sated with interest derived from observation of what Louise called "the earlier forms of life," which persevered with their bewildered little existences upon the gravel bottom. It was coming time for us to do our clumsy swimming in the water where a thousand million years before our ancestors had been at home; but we needed greater depth than they, and I set in train the construction of a new sluice.

My idea was to use a device which would be simpler than a sluice proper. I had in mind a drain-pipe-and-plug arrangement.

Harry George Pengelly tipped me off about some six-inch pipes, in twenty-four foot lengths, which had lain for many years in a field down in the gorge of the Teign. The farmer had once proposed to use them for some sort of hydro-electric scheme, but had no doubt decided that it would be less trouble to wait for the development of atomic energy. I bought a length of the pipe, and Harry George's nephew fetched it for me with his somersaulting Fordson.

I straightened and deepened the cut which had been the sluice outlet, and, with Bert's help, dropped in the pipe. We had saved up a tremendous quantity of old tins, garden refuse, and general rubbish, which I dumped into the cut, and finally filled it flush with the verge of the pond.

The position now was that we needed a plug for the six-inch pipe, whereupon the pond would fill. It had been my idea to have a tapered billet of beech to wedge in the pipe, which would have an iron staple into which one end of a lever would be inserted. The lever would be held on a fulcrum, so that when the top end was pulled the other would draw out the plug. Foolishly I contracted to have this bit of ironwork made up locally, instead of doing the fashioning myself, whereupon the usual merry-go-round was set in motion.

The first contractor to quote was persuaded to do so very quickly, for I caught him in the lane while he was driving from one job to another. He was shocked at this tampering with precedent, but in the end, like a judge in chambers, allowed himself to be interviewed on the subject under discussion, and finally, like a normal tradesman in any other county, to view the site of the proposed works, which was just over the hedge from his car.

He reckoned that 'tweren't much of a little old job, and that he knew just where some bits of iron was to, which would do properly, and would it be all right for a couple of his chaps to come up Monday, 8.30 A.M.?

I rang up on Monday fortnight, having given a week's grace, and, as frequently happened on these occasions, was answered by a woman who listened impatiently, as if the milk was boiling over while I kept her in dalliance, and pooh-poohed my story of the arrangement as a figment of a distorted imagination. To prove that I was either a knave or a fool she told me that the previous Monday had been the date for the start of a big job which her husband was undertaking for the Council; that he could not possibly have gone all out along to Shallows, therefore; neither could he for another fortnight, being fully occupied, but that if I wished him to carry out any work for me I might hope for his preliminary inspection on the third Monday hence; would 8.30 A.M. do?

My next arrangement was with one of the few small contractors within a reasonable radius with whom I had not had despairing relations at one time or another. This, as it turned out, was only because I had not before approached him. I now did so with great resolution, and to his surprise bullied him into making an immediate visit to view the pool. He reckoned that 'twouldn't be much of a little old job and that he knew just where a nice billet of wood was to, as he could turn for a plug for the six-inch pipe. I'd have to give 'un a two-three days to sort out bits and pieces un 'ould likely want, mind.

This I agreed to do, but on the fourth day, since June was now come and the children were plaguing for a swim, I telephoned. Why! exclaimed an anonymous voice. It couldn't say for sure when 'un 'ould be out Shallows 'cos 'un was away for a few days.

I tried again at the end of another week, and spoke to my contractor himself. He was, I thought, a little reproachful at this direct contact. He was certainly shocked when I inquired flatly whether he had made up the bit of ironwork, and turned the wooden plug, and if so why could he not come up instantly and fit the composite device. He hesitated for a moment, and I thought he was lost. Instead he knew his finest hour.

"Oh!" he said in an admonishing sort of voice. "Us can't get at it all slapdash like that, m'dear. Us'll have to find a day first for to come out there and measure diameter of six-inch pipe."

The next morning I cut a tapering plug of oak, tacked a layer of old carpet underfelt round it, and rammed it in the pipe. The pond was filled in forty-eight hours, and I pickaxed a hasty overflow to join that subterranean water-course beneath the lane which had carried also the full drainage of the pond when the sluice had been axed.

I had been a little incredulous of Hamish Drummond's tale of the prairie dew-ponds which had so quickly stocked themselves with eels, when the nearest supply was a day's train journey away. But now before our eyes we saw a more remarkable manifestation on the morning when we woke up to find a filled pool.

Louise was already teetering on the bank, wondering whether to jump or slide in, Johanna was standing in the shallow end; and Juno, barking nervously, obviously foresaw that she would find little pleasure in this new interest of her children. I retrieved the early bathers for breakfast, and when I went back to the pool with them afterwards found Rachel Hawkins' two young sons with a school friend all staring wistfully at the water from a vantage point in the lane. I could do none other than invite them in. Rachel Hawkins' gardener's two boys appeared at mid-morning, closely followed by two little girls from the ménage of Harry George Pengelly.

The noise was very considerable, since the young—and, indeed, many female adults—scream continuously during contact with cold water. There was further disturbance at lunch-time, because none of the visitors had been persuaded to return home, and we had to explain by telephone to resentful parents that the fault did not lie with us, but with a mass hysteria, which only a surfeit could exorcize. This prognostication led to the imposition of bans, which rendered sweeter the forbidden waters of the pool and thus endangered the Shallows relationships with less water-blessed houses, since their owners began to look upon the defection of their young as caused by deliberate efforts at alienation on our part.

However, on that inaugural day the machinery of parental control had only begun to creak by afternoon, and was not in the full flight of ponderous majesty. Thus all our morning visitors returned. They had scarcely entered the water and begun to scream when a strange young lady brought us to the door to inform us that Louise had made her acquaintance during one of her long rambles; that she was herself a girl guide in camp not very far away; and that the child had invited her and her companions to use the pool as their own as soon as it became ready. The young lady said simply that she noticed it was now ready.

We gave consent, and within the hour forty-two girls, young, pubescent, and waxing adult, led by a fierce captain who was on the wane, presented themselves. There was no question of two or three girls changing in the studio as we had envisaged. Girls changed in our bedroom and the children's, in the lavatory, bathroom, and sitting-room, and two in the greenhouse. I felt like Don Juan during that episode when he found himself sexually incognito in the seraglio. For, alone as I was among a litter of female undergarments, no one took note of me as I flitted from room to room in refuge from embarrassment, and finally into the rhododendron-bushes.

Thus our pool became at once a pleasure and a bane. It was a bane only because the quiet of the garden was shattered, but it was a pleasure apart from that disruption at all times and especially in the still of the dusk, and under the cold glim of the moon, at which times the water took on the warmth the air had lost. At these solitary hours we could slip into the water as unremarked as otters, and glide about our pool careful not to break the stillness with any splash from arms and legs. We could drift, too, in the small dinghy, as lonely as though we were castaways on the liquid desert of the great Pacific ocean. That the banks were but a few yards away mattered not at all at the magic hour. It sufficed that we were on water alone, untouchable, under the night sky.

From water we humans came, and never yet have we broken our bond with the element which, as our godmother, sponsored the christening of our family tree.

CHAPTER TWELVE

Tackling the wood—Moorland geology—Tin-streaming, mining, and china-clay working—The Stannary Parliament—Moor folk and the Duchy—Prehistory—November bonfire

MY expedition into the most inaccessible fastness within the wood, in order to control the stream which fed the pool, had left me with a determination to return. I did not wish to civilize those glades, those great clumps of shrubs and miniature waterfalls, but I did want to be able to go among them dry-shod and untorn by thorns.

Accordingly, that autumn, while Louise still swam daily as if she were at a duty, we began to tackle the wood in earnest.

I wonder if we were the first people to rip out by hand a bramble brake about three acres in extent. Here and there among myths, folklore, and the fairy tales which are descended from them, one hears the echoes of such tasks, set now and then to prove heroes and lovers. In the wood we proved our love of Shallows.

To some extent we used The Machine to cut into the barbed tangle, but this was no holiday for either of us. Our efforts were not typified by any of the cover designs on the many garden-tractor leaflets which Tessa and I had studied. We could not really visualize a slight honey-blonde in jeans by Huntsman bucketing any garden tractor through that fearful wilderness. The gallant little Machine did not lack courage or ability. It returned again and again to the attack, howling defiance. It tore into the brambles, the cutter-bar slicing those in front of it, together with the crop of saplings which grew through them. But we came to frequent halts, bound by the cut brambles and by the tentacles of those whose roots were out of reach, which wrapped themselves about and about each projection on The Machine, and round my body. Now and then the cutter-bar would slide under a fallen tree, lurking in

L

concealment in the undergrowth, and I would have to drag it back-ward to a clear space. There were clear spaces, for Tessa followed up behind me, raking and forking the fallen, prickly vines into heaps like victims of a pogrom ready for cremation.

For some weeks we cut and burned; we trimmed fallen timber, sawed it into lengths, and stacked it upright against living trees. All this was legitimate work. But I began to notice through the sweat that blinded me that Tessa was weeding as she followed behind me. I remonstrated at first, feeling that she would be better employed clearing up the debris than employing a delicate, window-box technique in a wilderness. But several times as I wearily re-tracted my steps at the end of the day I noticed that the ground over which I returned was not only raked clean but was cleared of the sturdy bramble stumps over which I was used to stumbling. I began to realize that there was fact behind the airy motto that the impossible takes but a little longer. In our wood it did not take much longer, for, though the run of vine from each root had deve-loped undisturbed until it and its supporters ran to a tremendous yardage, they had but the one root. We began to find that there were but thirty or forty roots in an area the size of a tennis-court, though it was impenetrable before The Machine tore into it. Thus, yard by yard, we cleared, burnt the useless, stacked the useful, and up-rooted the potential revivers of the former jungle.

The wood seemed to have to an even greater degree than the rest of the Shallows ground that illusion of illimitability. I do believe that to this day there are parts in which none of us has set foot, even though physical barriers no longer deny us access. Or perhaps we have been into these corners, along these miniature glades, up these diminutive river cañons, but do not remember them, haunted that they are.

The haunting of our wood is very old, and, fortunately, it is benign. During these more recent centuries the wood has formed a link between the scattered hamlet in which Shallows is and the moor. We, in our hamlet, are newcomers; the moor folk are our predeces-sors. They were predecessors of Norman, Angle, Roman, Celt, and Beaker Man, too.

Forty centuries ago the communities of Iberian migrants, early

Bronze folk, dwelt on the high tablelands below storm-swept mountain, but above the valleys, which were choked with timber and ranged by hunting beasts. Dartmoor was an area which teemed with human life and rang with its activity more than did any other part of Britain. The remains of the hut circles cluster thickly within a few hundred yards of the far end of our wood, and the avenues of standing stones draw enigmatic lines across the heather and set a question mark on many skylines.

Dartmoor is very old. The weather-polished tors, which break through its thin and tight-stretched skin of peat and earth, are the exposed backbone of a mountain range which once stretched thence south-westerly. The bared vertebrae lie open to the storm and sun across Bodmin Moor and at stark Lands End; they form the Isles of Scilly, flower-garlanded, before the restless sea decently covers them.

The softer rocks which were once piled up to form the Mountains of Armorica have gone. Some of their grandeur was whittled away by the attacks of the weather, but most of it was claimed by the seas beneath which the mountains were more than once dragged. At the last the granite backbone was laid bare; lies bare to this day; and is being worn down still. The acres of boulders which moor folk call 'clitters' lie beneath the tors like the dust of dissolution.

The marks of those ancient submarine submergences show not only negatively in the disappearance of softer rock strata, but positively in the old beaches, which remain. More than one such sinking was not complete, and the contours of the beaches show as wide, gently sloping shelves, with the steep scarp of sea-cliffs, carved by tides, rising at their back. One of these beaches of Tertiary times is now a thousand feet above sea-level, poised like a wide step below the riser to Kestor, and above that which drops to the valley of the Teign. Shallows is built on this old beach.

The run of the streams tells the story of the successive emergences of the moor from those warm primeval seas in which marine life was astir and multiplying; the life which was to lie throbbing on the margin where earth and water met, was to accustom itself to land, to herbage, and to flight through the air; the life from whose

continually rearranging cell patterns man was to result, either hap-
hazardly, or from deep purpose; the life which in man's form has
now at last attained that Himalayan peak whose summit is farthest
from its tidal cradle; the peak whose summit is set nearest the moon
and solar planets which are the next goals of man.

These Dartmoor streams amble quietly over the ocean-flattened
tableland of the moor, but plunge suddenly and swiftly down the
scarp, to dawdle again across the ancient beach which is now a
thousand feet above the waves which once smoothed and levelled it.
The streams have bitten deeply into the edges of the levels, just as a
running rope will chafe a groove in the edge of a board; and deep,
sometimes spectacular, gorges are cut, filled with moss-grown
boulders.

The spread of the glacial ice-caps was checked north of Dartmoor,
and the moor was spared the gouging progress of the majestic ice-
rivers which flowed from them. The valleys were not scoured out,
and the debris of the terminal moraines was not left to dam the
gorges. Thus there are no natural lakes on Dartmoor, such as lend
enchantment in Cumberland and Westmorland and a mixture of
beauty and savagery as in Wales. The moor was able to shed its
water without hindrance, as sea runs off a surfaced whale.

The granite core of Dartmoor has not only left the typical tors
weather-carved to resemble piles of giant crystals, but has profoundly influenced man's relation to the moor. For the rock has
held many desirable substances, and attracted many searchers as
far back as the times of prehistory.

Granite is an igneous rock, once molten in the fires which
attended the birth pangs of the recognizable world. The liquid
cooled, and crystallized deep below the surface under the vast pres-
sures of the tormented crust. There are quartz, feldspars, mica, and
a small percentage of minerals in granite. These minerals were the
earliest attraction which brought man in numbers: tin, copper, zinc,
iron, and traces of silver and gold.

Most schoolboys have heard of the Phœnician voyages to the
Armorican peninsula to obtain tin. A regular trade between the
West Country and the Mediterranean undoubtedly existed through
many pre-Christian centuries, and I believe that the Phœnician is to

be seen in many Cornish folk of to-day. And, lest anyone boggles at my present recognition of ancient seafarers whose physical attributes are arguable, let him read of the Phœnicians and judge their character by the actions told of in history, and measure the modern Cornishman against those historic Phœnician characteristics.

Most likely the tin of Devon and Cornwall was first won by streaming. The men of the early Bronze Age, nearly four thousand years ago, probably worked the streams, seeking slow-flowing reaches where the heavy tin-bearing stones tended to rest on the bed. The waste of the panning was thrown on the banks, and may be seen to-day in grass-grown heaps along many Dartmoor rivulets.

The mining probably came later. It was a way of extraction which was only worth while in the richer veins and which called for some organization and plant. Much of the Dartmoor mining, more perhaps than that of Cornwall, was by the open-cast method. Often enough Tessa and the children and I have found ourselves in some deep gully, heedless at first, but coming to a revelation that this was no water-worn ravine, but the desperate work of an earlier race, struggling to win currency for a luxury or two. "Plus ça change, plus c'est la même chose."

It may be that the primitive tin-workers burned much wood in their smelting process and thus denuded the moor. Most likely they burned some, provided it was near the scene of their operations, but I do not believe that Dartmoor was ever extensively afforested. There are few traces of trees preserved in the peat. It is more probable that it was this peat which was mostly used.

The granite skeleton of the moor was not left fully protected by the skin of peat, grown whin, heather, and witches' oaks. Subterranean spasms set up complex strains; Plutonian emanations seeped upward, and climatic percolations soaked downward. Many complex factors worked upon the feldspar content of the granite, initiating a process of disintegration, of rotting, which ended in the depositing of kaolin. It is from these kaolin deposits that china clay is won.

But the working of china clay came very much later in the moor's history than did tin-streaming and mining, and its influence has been more ephemeral. Mining has always been a developer of a typical character: a character where independence is mingled with forthrightness to the point of rudeness, and with suspicion to the point of aloofness. Under a similar veneer of charm to that of the Southern Irish, many native Devonians to-day camouflage the inherited tin-miners' character. The Cornishman, by the way, uses no camouflage. The tin-miners did not individually nurse the peculiarities of their respective characters, but consolidated them. In Norman times they won recognition for their ways of working, and for their own Stannary Parliament, whose powers rested upon the four Stannary towns, of which Rattleford was one.

The miners were specifically granted the right by Henry III to take peat, called coal, for their furnaces. They exercised the power to mine where they wished, even in a man's private plot, and were thus forerunners in spirit of our present Coal Board. They laid down regulations as to who might enter their industry, foreshadowing the closed-shop principle.

However, the Stannary Parliament, although as autocratic as a shop-stewards' convention, did closely check the quality of their product, guaranteeing its purity, and stamping it with a brand which may be called a cross between hall-mark and trademark.

The immediate history of the moor folk—that is, the history during the last millenium—is that of squatting, either by families or communities. This squatting was but a nibbling at the fringe of the heather blanket; a fight to tame a few enclosed acres to forgetfulness of the wild. As often as not, like reverted to like, and rush and heath imperturbably reclaimed their own, and allowed no more than the tumbled and half-covered stones of a wall to lie as the monument to the buried hope and endeavour of a lifetime.

Settled holdings on the moor proper are few indeed, and the vast majority of them are found clinging to the slope which falls in folds and creases, like a wind-billowed curtain, from the high plateau to the moat of lowland. The higher holdings are balanced along the thousand-foot contour, and at this altitude their occupiers just maintain equilibrium between the defences thrown up by their labours and the weight of the moor's infiltrating attack.

The rights of grazing and peat-cutting, which appear in the deed of Shallows under the more romantic names of venville and turbary, are of shadowy origin. Through the reigns of the early Normans Dartmoor was known as a 'forest': a title which indicates a royal hunting domain, rather than a wood. When Henry III passed the ground to his brother Richard, Duke of Cornwall, it ceased to be Crown property, and became known as a 'chase.' Yet so far was the moor from the purlieus of Court, and so far removed, as was all the West Country, was it from the main lines of communication, that little enough princely attention was given it. The tinners pursued their individual way, the squatters challenged the hostility of soil and climate, and the royal claims to verte and venison were not much respected. In any case, deer have never thrived on the moor.

The history of moorland grazing is a long tale of bickering between commoners and Duchy. To this day many a loyal Queen's man about Rattleford will spit, and declare, "Duchy's pigs!"

I do not think that the executives of the Duchy have ever done any commoner much harm, not even in older times of royal perogative, yet dislike has grown, and remains at least as bitter as it ever was.

The real forest is a strip in the centre of the moor, some ten miles by twenty, which runs from north to south on a line between Oke-hampton and Ivybridge. The much larger area which surrounds the forest is divided into the various commons, their limits often marked by standing stones and impressed upon the young each seven years at the ceremony of beating the bounds.

Yet over the whole moor, forest, and common, the graziers do much as they please. They ignore the old laws of levancy and couchancy, which demanded the withdrawal of all beasts between sunset and sunrise; they ignore the custom which allowed a man to graze only that number of beasts which the produce of his culti-vated holding could feed in winter. They cut hags and peat as they will; they take stone and gravel on payment of but a nominal royalty, and that paid only rarely. They may burn the vegetation at will, even though indiscriminate and uninstructed swaling destroys more potential growth than it encourages.

To all these activities the Duchy tacitly accedes, as if it knows in its heart that its own rights are clouded by doubt. Yet it has equally tacitly slipped on the cloak of overlordship, and dare not have it ripped off, nor too often muddied without that it loses dignity. Sometimes, therefore, it is forced to act with diffidence, lest its own rights be called in question. There have been modern instances of land enclosure by squatters; and of those feats of house-building between sunrise and sunset, which have ever been supposed to confer title, but by what precedent no one can state. In some of these instances the Duchy has demanded and won a peppercorn rent. The Duchy's honour was satisfied, and the squatters, none too sure of either their physical or legal grounds, were well content to pay a pittance to avoid a courtroom airing.

However, neither the ancient royal nor later quasi-royal power ever made the absolute demands of the twentieth-century's ministries. The civil servant has enclosed larger tracts than any king proposed for his own use. The Forestry Commission has planted five thousand acres of conifers; the War Office retains thirty-two thousand acres as an artillery range. One can be sorry about these encroachments, which have absorbed a good quarter of the remaining moorland, without denying the necessity for them.

Until man crosses the oceans of inter-stellar space he has no living adversary but himself. By tribes and nations, by religions and creeds, by colour and custom, he has lined up his order of battle. Perhaps the sects of humanity will never be ranged on the one side until they can make common cause. Such unison may not be found in any earthly purpose of war or peace, but only in an enterprise greater than any yet attempted, and in meeting the dangers which may be provoked. Until then by nations we train for war so that prowess at arms may be the deterrent of subjugation and death. We must not grudge those forbidden acres on Dartmoor which may yet pay a high dividend.

I am one who likes conifers in the upland landscape, despite the criticism that they are not native to it; that if any tree has a place on moor and mountain it is the hardwood. I only hold it against the plantations that throughout these islands so many have been grown upon ground which might have been reclaimed for farm cropping.

These considerations are not the ones which most move us at Shallows. It is not the history of this half-century, nor of a dozen centuries before it, which most fills our minds. We think most of the tale which the moor tells of its dwellers of two thousand years ago, and of another two thousand years before that. It tells a tale of Neolithic, Bronze Age, and Iron Age man, whose doings and thoughts are the pre-natal influences which still much sway that precocious offspring, Atomic man. Some people deny that the moor has any atmosphere except that compounded of its wildness and loneliness. Wild it is, but the loneliness is only that of a much used room, recently left by its tenants. The air of close occupancy lingers, and its litter remains in the form of a host of barrows, hut circles, and long stone avenues, laboriously and industriously set up when the moor was probably the most thickly peopled part of these islands.

There have been found few traces of the pre-Bronze Age dwellers; a handful of Mesolithic flint weapon heads and tools, and a larger quantity from Neolithic days. But there is almost no pottery or other indication of the drift of peoples across that ill-lit distant stage. The peat layer is too thin to have held safely such keepsakes of the past; its acid property eats into substance, and its wetness crumbles it.

That which remains to tell of the busy people who lived thickly above our house, and not far from the edge of the wood, is the natural stone of the moor, ranged and set up for an ancient purpose and a modern monument. It is most likely that the majority of these hut circles, pounds, stone circles, and avenues were set up by the Bronze Age people, who may, I think, have improved upon and multiplied cruder Megalithic structures which they found in being.

These Bronze Age migrants, who came in successive waves from the eastern Mediterranean fringes, knew the secret of metal working, and I dare say they ferreted out the moor's treasure of tin, and settled there to work it. In those days, nearly four thousand years ago, much of the low-lying ground in these islands was made up either of dense forests or swamp. It was unhealthy, almost uncultivable, short of grazing, and the haunt of wild beasts.

As a result, the settled habitations of communal life were concentrated on those uplands which offered a compromise between hostile jungle and storm-swept mountain. It was on these uplands that the small dark Iberian migrants settled.

Of all the populous Bronze Age areas, Dartmoor was probably the most isolated. It remained, perhaps, a backwater into which new currents filtrated but slowly. Possibly its inhabitants were working the lovely bronze long after iron had usurped the lordship of the lowlands and had facilitated a beginning of their clearance. And, in turn, when iron at last found a place in the usages of the moor late-comers to these islands—Brythonic Celts, Belgæ, and Romans—probably found the moor men to be strange and addicted to old ways.

It is likely that strangers found the moor men frightening, and perhaps uncanny. Their religious rites must indeed have been secretive, since no whisper of their form has breathed on the pages of history. Their beehive huts of lichened stone, turf-roofed, were often part sunk in the ground; they were no more than humps in the heather, entered by a low dark passage through whose aperture a hastening traveller might hear voices speak in a strange tongue. It was easy on his return to tell tales of the small dark people who flitted between the boulders of the clitters and vanished into the ground before one's very eyes. It may be, too, that a benighted wayfarer did not always return to the valley to tell such a tale, and I dare say some lowland rhymester said in paraphrase:

> Up the airy mountain,
>   Down the rushy glen,
> We daren't go a-hunting,
>   For fear of little men.

Some modern archæologists believe that the ring of forts about the approaches to the moor were not thrown up by the little men to ward off intruders, but that Iron Age man, busy at carving out his lowland holdings from jungle, built them to restrain incursions from a Bronze Age remnant which survived on the high ground.

There is pathos in the speculative story. On the moor of a night, when the dark trees of Shallows were no more than a pool of shadow below me, I have imagined a dying fragment of a race; an anachronism, hemmed in, feared, and themselves frightened. During several centuries before B.C. became A.D. the climate of Britain worsened drastically, and I have imagined our moor men perished and famished, dying a racial death of the hereditary effects of cold and damp, unable to stay where they were if they hoped to survive, and unable, perhaps, to descend to the valleys without meeting a swifter death at the hands of fellow men. Man had by now become a surer killer, a deadlier enemy than the elements.

Thus, maybe, the little dark people of the moor perished by the cruelty of both climate and iron-tipped spear. All that remains, giving me the impression of an indefatigable business, are their long stone rows, circles, and pounds, and the humped barrows of their dead. To me the moor is as resonant with echoes as the pavements and halls of a sacked city.

We have sat, the children and I, within the perimeter wall of Grimspound; sat within a hutment inside the great wall, and have imagined much that may have been true happenings. And within the lonely Gidleigh circle, not so many miles away, we have felt less homely thoughts; seeing in the eye of our minds a reflection ofthe religious emotions in which the standing stones are steeped.

The moor is not an empty place, but there are upon it some desperately lonely souls.

Thus, perhaps, it was understandable that we felt a special significance in our wood on that very first November that we had a cleared way to the outpost trees which kept watch on the moor. We had an immense bonfire, and in those surroundings the flames which made a cave of light under the weight of darkness played an older ritual.

This season was the Celtic New Year; it was Guernsey's Bout de l'An; it was the original date of Hogmanay. Nature had taught pastoral man that now was the time of the New Year, when the last leaves fell; the grasses turned brown; hibernation began; and the flocks and herds were brought from the high ground, just as they are to-day. This was the greatest and oldest ceremonial of them all; it was the prehistoric November fire festival of Samhain, when the dying year was burned, and the infant year was warmed by the funeral pyre. This pointed the lesson of animal and inanimate existence, that death nourishes life in an endless cycle.

The Church had long frowned upon the rites of Samhain, carried unthinkingly into Christian days until the Puritans imposed the final ban. But so deep-rooted an observance was but suppressed, not exorcized. When Guido Fawkes so closely failed to blow up his Protestant royal family, bishops, and Parliament with a ton and a half of gunpowder, the common people readily used the excuse so painfully provided by the tortured Guido on so fortuitous and coincidental a date. Were they really burning Guido on their bonfires? Or did the dying year lie under his effigy?

The burning was a most inaccurate reminder of the escape of princes and Parliament, and of the punishment of the chief plotter. For Guido Fawkes was hanged.

This ancient New Year was not a celebration of a night, a perfunctory mark of the most important moment in the annual cycle, when the seeds were scattered and life, invisible as yet, had been conceived anew in the womb of the earth, and awaited its quickening in the spring season. At this time was the night of All Souls. At this nadir of the year the barrier between the living and the dead became less determinate. The Church has grafted, as so often it has, its own usage on more ancient practice, and on this night remembers the great concourse of the dead. But in older days, and in days more recent than many know, people were not content with dim remembrance. Families would sit the night through, straining to reach across the gulf to whose farthest edge their dead had crowded. They would set a candle in each window of the listening house to be a guide and welcome through the darkness. They would eat the Soul Cakes, specially baked; and they would not forget the needs of those visitors for whom they waited fearfully, but left food and wine to put body into such shades as might venture. For the dead can no more than squeak like bats unless they are nourished. It was Odysseus who gave them power to speak, through the virtue in goblets of blood.

All Souls was banished by the reformers of the Church of England, afraid of the strength of pre-Christian custom which it carried, and the ceremonial did not reappear until 1928.

Intertwined with All Souls and the Old New Year was the eve of All Hallows, the night of spooks and witches, to whose ritual has at some time been joined attempts at divination which may themselves be caricatures of Druidic soothsaying; and the soothsaying in turn was most probably based on the rites of prophecy which the Hamitic migrants brought to Britain from the land and the era of the Old Testament.

Those who to-day play the games of Hallowe'en, who throw the apple-peel over their shoulder to read in its fall the initials of a future lover, are parodying the sacrificial divination of the Eastern Mediterranean ancients Those who bob for apples bow their heads to a pre-Israelite worship, to the reverence of the rosy orb as the symbol of unending life.

We return wittingly, we moderns, to many of these old blind beliefs, but rarely give credit to the accurate instincts of those who travelled the rim of the circle so long before us, and so less well equipped. It is but recently that scientific thought postulates that light, space, and time may flow in an endless curve.

That first November that the wood was cleared Tessa and I stayed late beside our fire night after night through the bonfire season. The children waited with us while darkness stalked from the trees to lay his cloak over the moor. On to the flames we piled more and yet more of the litter which marked a score of seasons, as the lines of seaweed mark the rhythm of the high tides, which also follow the beat of the orchestration of the spheres.

Those small dark men of the moor had laid their avenues at the dictation of the sun, and their rituals too were enacted at the landmarks of earth's voyage about the source of warmth and life. It seemed to me sometimes that they came quietly down the slope to stand just beyond the trees, the dangers of whose deeper dark instinctively they feared. Like that of most things at Shallows, their presence was actively kindly and unresentful of our intrusion into a place whose past vibrated with the echoes of events. But, after all, the scene in the November wood was not strange to them; though they knew nothing of Guy Fawkes, they knew all about the great fires of Samhain.

CHAPTER THIRTEEN

*Holly—The scavenger—Midland market—A feast for the birds
—Gift boxes—Covent Garden success—Poltergeist—Chanterelles
and other fungi*

JUST after we had moved down to Shallows, about six weeks before Christmas, the country spivs descended upon us in search of holly. Their patter was much the same at the several visitations.

"Plenty about this year. Best let's have your bit before the birds get at the berries. Give yer a coupler quid, guv'ner, and me an' me mate'll do the work."

This latter promise we regarded as being really a threat to our trees, and we pictured a trail of devastation, as well as a snapping up of unconsidered trifles, as me-an'-me-mate moved about the place. At the same time Tessa was most anxious to achieve a Christmas dinner at the expense of the garden, for even in those early days she desired the satisfaction of teaching it to earn its keep.

She is still not discouraged, hope springing as eternally as the seasons wax and wane.

Tessa remembered well the half-crown sprigs of holly on sale in London, just as during our first spring she was to recall the seventeen-shillings-and-sixpenny sprays of azalea blossoms in Mayfair, such as we were to present to chance acquaintances in Rattleford not by the spray but by the car load. Before that first Christmas the wood was difficult to enter save in one or two parts, but on an early tour of inspection Tessa estimated that there was a hundred sovereigns' worth of holly accessible to us, provided it was translated to metropolitan markets. We wrote off, therefore, to one or two Covent Garden firms, and in our imaginations laid out the windfall of a hundred pounds while we awaited the replies. The replies stated simply that the respective firms had made their arrangements some considerable time previously.

Thus, when the ultimate spiv turned up at the door we looked on him with kindly eyes. He was, in any case, a nice-looking little man, like a robin in appearance, wearing corduroys, a traditional red spotted neckerchief, and a felt hat with the crown undented. A woman, his mate we assumed, hopped about uncertainly beside the runt of a sawn-off lorry in which they had driven up.

He had, he said, bought regularly from Shallows, knew his way about, and did not hurt the trees. We bargained for a bit, then settled for no less than a five-pun note, him and his missus to do the cutting, beginning next day. I glanced in the back of the little lorry before it exploded down the drive, and read therein the daily task. The lorry contained two iron bed ends, those universal objects about the countryside, which, when their time as head-and-foot-stones to mark the bed of procreation and birth is done, are used to fill a gap in a hedge, deputize for a gate, reinforce concrete, and build the foundation of a rick. There was a sheepskin; a pile of rabbit skins; about six couples of snared rabbits; a bundle of empty bran bags, which at that time were worth two shillings apiece; some completely unidentifiable lumps of very solid old iron; and a bag of sphagnum moss, which our acquaintance told me was destined to feed orchids. There was an attractive flavour to the outfit which was, somehow, more wholesome than that of the urban persons who officially call themselves general dealers. Our cheery little man may well have filled a useful purpose in exchanging a little of his cash for a lot of junk, and introducing the junk to persons who had some unguess-able needs for it. The scavenger, in his many guises, is indispensable.

We were not to be caught out by tardiness in our second winter at Shallows, and so made arrangements in good time to deliver our holly to a stall-holder in a Midlands city market who had been well recommended to us. All of us got to work at cutting, each with a pair of pruners. We had plenty of those tools, since we were ever losing them, hunting for them till hope died, buying anew in the end, then finding one or more lost pairs. After a while we had about half a dozen pairs in circulation on the principle of army socks: one pair on, one in me locker, one in the wash, sir. With our pruners it was usually two pairs with Tessa and me, two on the hooks by the back door, and two lost in the bushes. The children were helping because they had been cut in on a percentage basis, their arithmetic becoming surprisingly good during the discussion and their demeanour being that of two characters from Damon Runyon.

We had by now learned a little about the marketing of holly. It appeared that the early demand was created by the wreath-makers who catered for the human love of symbolism, expressed in this case by the offering of greenery on the winter graves as the symbol of resurrection and everlasting life. The wreath-makers must have made quite a good thing of it. Although we did not have many variegated hollies, and these were always reluctant berriers, the unadorned leaves were acceptable to these artists, being used for special effects, with wired on berries, if necessary.

It was sprigs, rather than sprays, which were demanded for this churchyard market: twigs rather than branches. But though the grower lost the weight of thick wood in his consignment, he was said to be compensated by the high price of well-berried sprigs.

Our Midlands merchant had promised to send us boxes. Painfully through the frost we carried our loads of holly into a linhay ready for the packing, while the children estimated and re-estimated their dues. But no boxes came, and despite our care to harvest in good time that year, the days of December added to their tally. We blamed the railways system, the ice-bound roads, and the stall-holder in natural priority, and, as sometimes is the case, found the last at fault. An expensive telephone call produced a voluble but barely intelligible man who was delighted to tell us the story of his life, trace the development of the Black Country, and make a market survey for only a shilling a minute of our money. In the end our acquaintance swung skilfully round in a verbal circle, explaining at the end of the market survey that, since ready money was tight, the wastage in flower-boxes was not now made good; that, owing to the hotch-potch growth and absence of planning of Black Country communications, an undue percentage of such boxes as existed were in transit at any given time; finally, returning to his starting-point, we would appreciate from what he had told us of his early home life, religious convictions, and business principles, that he was a man of his word or as near as he could get. He had, therefore, sent us by passenger train a bundle of sacks.

Thus was the fresh brightness of green and scarlet holly staled and dimmed. In the late market it returned us much less than it should. Even so we received nearly a shilling a pound net on two hundredweight of sprigs, and the children, at any rate, were satisfied. We too felt at the back of our minds that we had glimpsed the possibilities of a productive garden.

The following year we again made selling arrangements in good time, but while we watched with satisfaction the deepening colour of the berries the birds too must have been arranging and watching. At some avian signal they swarmed in from every copse and wooded glen within several hundred yards, blackbirds and thrushes predominating; robins joined in angrily, each with those trespassers who had invaded his corner of the garden; and the buzzard hawk, who had become more or less a fixture on the gable of the garage, watched amiably over all. The trees were stripped within forty-eight hours, except one or two orange-berried types whose fruit never fully ripened until January.

I have seen birds act similarly with a cherry-tree, feigning not only indifference, but ignorance that the tree existed, or, alternatively, that they felt an aversion to its fruit. Then, as if a gong had been beaten, they would swoop like boarding-house guests, gobbling the lot in a flurry of elbows.

Next year the holly never berried at all. At least, we managed to find enough to decorate the house sparingly, and to send a few boxes of sprigs to town friends. Tessa, determined not to let the trees lapse into financial barrenness, whatever their fruiting state, felt that these gift boxes were just the present for those friends in between the intimate ones who do not so much as rank a card and the comparative strangers who must be given a guinea's worth of something useless.

We received so warm a response to our holly parcels that we have ever since kept up the custom, widening the circle of recipients.

I suppose the gift of holly evokes particular gratitude because of its very personal nature. There were our sprays of laquered green and polished red, shining with the brittle glitter of the frost crystals

M

which had so recently besprinkled them; they were undimmed by soot, as fresh as the north wind, clean as the moorland scent. I believe they really breathed purity into the dishonoured city air.

Our holly must have played an important part in the intimacy of family Christmas; as a welcoming wreath on the outer door; in hall, sitting-room, and bedroom; and at dinner with all the ceremony of a will-o-the-wisp blue flame and aroma of brandy butter.

The origin of holly is personal, also, for it is much too unpredictable a tree to be dragooned by the professional grower. In some years that of a whole district will be unberried, and anyone who by chance has an odd tree well-fruited will be counting on the scarcity value of the sprigs. But most likely the holly of the districts surrounding will be weighed down with berries, and the famine an illusion. The generative habits of holly are as mysterious as its mythology; of the inconspicuous white flowers which it bears in summer, some are male and some female. Yet pollination does not always seem to bring fruitfulness, as if either the male flowers are sterile or the female barren. Further to infuriate the commercially minded grower, a tree may suddenly decide to become a hermaphrodite.

As a result of these mischievous feints and follies, the gathering of holly is largely the business of the amateur; of the thousands of country folk who pick at irregular intervals of years according to the local lack or profusion of berries. The townsman often pins up with his spray a rural hope for an extra shilling or two to buy some unwonted luxury; his decoration is sometimes the prize of a pleasantly illegal deed of childish daring.

The candles, greenery, gifts, and mutual goodwill of this Christmas season are customs which, like so many of our festivals, are rooted in prehistory. The Roman Saturnalia were celebrated on December 17 of the old calendar, with just these very candles, decorations, and gifts, and were marked by the masters waiting upon their slaves. And the Saturnalia were themselves sprung from the primitive feast of the winter solstice.

The pagan Teuton tribes, at this darkest time of the north European year, used to hang evergreens in their dwellings as refuges for weather-plagued wood-sprites.

There are parts of England—Derbyshire notably—where the prickly holly is known as 'he,' and the gentle as 'she.' It is maintained that man or wife will prevail for a twelvemonth according to which is hung. Just in case there was, as so often there is, a grain of truth to back this belief Tessa and I tried to mix the contents of our gift parcels of holly. We had no wish to be responsible for domestic disharmony.

It was at our fourth attempt at marketing that we achieved considerable success. We had made very early arrangements with a Covent Garden wholesaler, and received from him half a dozen wooden flower-boxes about three feet six inches by eighteen inches by six inches in depth. By mid-November the garden and woodland were gay with berries. We held off from picking as long as we could, scanning the sky for the clouds of birds as anxiously as dive-bombed soldiers ever looked for Stukas. Our nerve broke at last, and we hurriedly filled our six boxes during the last week of the month.

We cut berried sprigs, many not more than nine inches long, which just suited the wreath-makers. It suited us, too, to take as little wood as possible from the trees, for holly is a slow grower. We packed a weight of about six pounds into each box and sent them off by passenger train. Our man telegraphed next day that our samples had returned us eight shillings a box net. We, in turn, telegraphed for a hundred more boxes.

In the end we received a net return which worked out at about fifteen pence a pound. I cannot think of many other wild crops, amateur gathered, which show a like return in considerable bulk.

The holly is very versatile. It has a hard, even-grained timber which is white and smooth enough to simulate ivory. Alternatively, it may be stained in order to become ebony teapot handles. However, one must be careful when felling a whole gentle holly-tree, for one may thereby release a poltergeist.

We first learned of the dangers of this during the early days of the War. Tessa was lodging at a house on the fringe of Salisbury Plain which was known as Holly-tree Farm. Another wife, whose husband was, like me, performing desperate deeds on the Plain, was a fellow lodger. It happened that Holly-tree Farm was built in the very angle of a ninety-degree road bend, its garden flimsily fenced, and at the apex of the angle was the house's godmother, the holly-tree.

Tessa became distressed at the demeanour of her fellow lodger, who often stood pale and drawn watching the insouciance with which the service drivers swung round the bend. As more and more vehicles came on unit establishment, and bren carriers and even tanks became commoner, the poor woman went into a decline.

It appeared that she feared for the destruction of the holly-tree, whose bark was already bruised. A playful tap from a tank would certainly have been too much for it. Tessa gathered that she and her husband had ignorantly felled a gentle holly at their pre-War home, and had instantly been beset by an imp who had taken over a specific half of the house. To that day, only the—so to speak—unoccupied half of the house was let. The lady was in dread that, in the event of accident, it would be her half of Holly-tree Farm that the new poltergeist would requisition.

It would be unfair to say that the Shallows garden was naturally unproductive, except for the holly and the nettle and dandelion leaves which were our vegetable stand-by after the annual bullock raid. But its production was as unexpected as the big holly cheque had been. For instance, we had long admired a fungus which grew in the wood, though we admired from a distance with the correct measure of British caution for such a growth. It was a delicate fungus, which began like a flat button, and grew to resemble an apricot-coloured sunshade, blown inside out. The ribs fluted up the stem and carried on along the umbrella part. It was very pretty in its clusters, as are many growths which are as poisonous as the wicked stepmother's rosy apple. Such seems to be Nature's inherent lure to destruction.

After an absence from home of a few days, I was horrified to find Tessa at work in the kitchen on a great heap of these perilous apricot-tinted fungi. It appeared that some Austrian friends had recently called, and had seen the fungi during a walk in the wood. They had run towards them with glad cries, and had speedily filled hats, handkerchiefs, and kirtled skirts. Tessa had learned that these fungi were chanterelles.

Louise took me outside and explained that she did not wish to alarm Johanna, but was I quite sure that Mother knew what she was about? Johanna then announced that she desired to whisper a secret and stated flatly in a very loud hissing tone that we would all die if we partook of the heap on the kitchen table, but that we must hurt nobody's feelings by refusing.

I studiously gave the appearance of a man with an open mind, and told the children of unusual but delicious courses such as bird's-nest soup, shark's fins, plovers' eggs, snails, frogs, hedgehogs, larks' tongues, and minnow tansy. They listened with polite interest, but reverted to the question of protocol. What if Mother, after taking so much trouble, offered openly to poison the rest of the family? Would it be a breach of etiquette to declare an inclination to live? Or would a white lie be justified—such as a sudden and griping stomach pain?

Meanwhile Tessa had melted some butter—probably euphemistic margarine—in a saucepan, and had shovelled in the beautiful, if treacherous, fungi. A lot of juice came out, which she thickened with flour. In a short while she added some stock, and while the witches' brew simmered a most appetizing smell permeated the kitchen. So appetizing was it that I could not help but taste the mound of fungus which at last appeared on a full round of toast. The original peach-apricot colour was, of course, gone, but a subtle apricot aroma remained, and an equally subtle flavour which resembled nothing I knew, unless, again, it were very refined apricots.

The children fidgeted for a while with their knives and forks, watching my attitude change from deepest suspicion, through acquiescence, to great pleasure. Presently they began to pick at their helping, not, I am sure, because they felt it their duty to follow me into the unknown, but because they were hungry, the dish smelt delicious, and Father was still alive after eating all he could get. We never looked askance after that first sampling, except to rue the years before, which had been empty of chanterelles.

Now that the scales were fallen from our eyes we remembered a deep and spectacular gorge of the infant Teign, not a mile from Shallows, where in the past we had seen quantities of chanterelles.

Here, in tearing haste in its plunge from the moorland plateau, the young river had gashed the step which was the ancient beach on which our house was built, and had chafed a cleft a couple of hundred feet deep. The gorge was filled with trees, the roots of succeeding ranks in line with the tops of those below. Here was indeed a haunted place, uneasy by daylight, actively evil at dusk. What emotions of hatred and fear had first set off those dread virbrations I have never found out, for the moor keeps its history more secret than any part of Britain. Some event of a horror unusual even in man's inhuman past had taken place down here. However, the chanterelles grew there in profusion. They had another advantage over the mushroom in addition to flavour, for they cropped twice a year—in spring and again in autumn. Now that our insular fungoid inhibition was charmed away, we sought other delicacies of the genus. We tried Poor Man's Beefsteak, that vast growth which is parasitic on both dead and living trees; and the smaller pearl-grey oyster fungus. Both were gastronomically dull. We discovered the delicious morel, most prized of fungi, which varies in colour from black to brown, and whose cap is made up of a honeycomb structure like foam rubber. Similar in structure to the morel, and growing in profusion in the haunted gorge, was another fungus which our Austrians named *Butterlinger*. Its honeycomb was covered by a skin the exact shade of caramel and was sticky as though such a sauce had been poured over it. The children took to devouring quantities fried for breakfast.

So fond have we become of chanterelles that we have dug from the Teign gorge square blocks of the leaf-mould in which the most prolific clusters flourished, and which must be impregnated with spores. These blocks we have inserted in the mould of our wood, and now wait to see whether we will increase our own native crop.

However, fungi are as unpredictable as the primitive so often is; as mysterious in their habits as the aborigine. They are a genus which is difficult to place in a category, and all that the many species have in common is a negative quality: lack of chlorophyll, the green substance which absorbs the virtues of sunlight to nourish vegetable growth. Because they are denied the help of the sun, fungi must feed on such growths as are not so denied, and they have become either parasites or saprophytes, feeding upon live or dead matter. The parasites are a danger to husbandry, for they attack crops. The rust fungus battens upon wheat; potato blight is the result of a fungoid infection; and so is the damping-off of seedlings; and mildew and mould.

But many of the saprophytes try to make up for these depredations, and act as busy scavengers, eating up undesirable waste products, just as does the common fly of the East. Then there are the Slime Fungi, which are really rather pleasant little objects with a much nicer proper name of Mycetozoa, or fungus animals. These move in search of their food, digesting it in a sort of primitive kidney; and reproducing their kind by division, like amœbæ.

Nature draws a careful balance sheet, and while some of the Mycetozoa clear up a lot of waste for us, others attack living organisms. The Plasmodiophora, for instance, fussy feeders, enjoy only the Brassica family of plants, cabbages and the like, and their ravenings are known as club-root. However, it is not the big umbrella of mushroom or chanterelle which is of importance in botanobiology, to coin a science for the fungi, for the cap is no more than a spore-producing body. It is the threadlike spores, the mycelium, which are the active organisms, penetrating the soil in search of decaying vegetable-matter.

The commercial mushroom spawn is no more than dried matter impregnated with mycelium, just like the chunks of leaf mould which we have dug out of the gorge of the Teign to insert in the mould of our wood.

CHAPTER FOURTEEN

*The peat set—Bill Waters—Difficulties: rough tracks, weather,
and lack of capital—The tramway—The granulator—Unfriendly
moor—The end of three years' work*

T HERE was a reason for our purchase of Shallows, though the
train of causation which led us to the house was very long.
We were set upon our way one winter evening in London, where we
were living and experiencing the post-war anticlimax. That
particular night Tessa and I were introduced to a man who took, it
seemed, great interest in us, and who drew from me whatever I
knew of rural ways and upland country, and who presently
inquired most delicately into my financial position. Within a week
our new acquaintance put to us a business proposition which was
in bucolic contrast to the sophisticated surroundings of our Chelsea
home. It was that we should join with him in the working of a
three-hundred-acres Dartmoor peat set, of which he had the lease
of twenty-eight years from the Duchy of Cornwall, and to which I
was to contribute the necessary capital.

This was, at any rate, an excuse for Tessa and me to visit a
county which we scarcely knew, and we drove down one cold grey
December day. The following morning, under the guidance of my
potential partner, we turned up a track which led from the Oke-
hampton-to-Tavistock road. The track climbed quietly over the
billows of the moor. It was a rutted stony way, in parts no more
than two gravel runnels through the heather, and as we mounted
towards the hem of the mist curtain the track became a shelf which
slanted up the side of a gorge which had been cut deeply and steeply
by the stream which we could see foaming down below us. Presently the mist enfolded us, stiffling the noise of our going, silencing
our voices, and detaching us from our surroundings. Here and
there the track had been washed out by flooding rivulets, and here

and there frost-prised boulders lay on it. When we had travelled blindly for four miles we came to the flat moorland plateau, whose height is a little below two thousand feet, and after we had run on the level for a short distance Tessa and I were surprised to see a big stone building loom more solid than the mist.

Our Chelsea guide, who answered to the name of Sol, took over. He explained that the works had been put up many years ago to process peat, extracting from it the many chemicals which it contained, and experimenting in the production of other possible derivatives, such as fuel for internal combustion engines. Now the great walls of dressed granite were a monument, and perhaps a warning. The track ended at the building, and we walked into a wide cutting, which was floored with the crunching, rotted granite which can betoken the presence of kaolin and china clay. We learned that there was indeed said to be china clay beneath the peat which lay untouched eight to twelve feet deep on either side of our cutting.

Sol had brought a spade with him, and we sliced away the weather-crumbled face of the peat wall until we could see its natural make-up in the cross-section, like a cut layer-cake. On top was the skin of root-bound turf; next, the light brown peat, so fibrous that it was difficult to tear in the hands, but shading to a darker colour deeper down and becoming less tough in texture; and at last, resting on the granite floor, was a four-foot layer of deep peat whose consistency was that of black butter, and into which one could drive the spade up to the handle with the pressure of a couple of fingers.

It was impressive, this cross-sectioned view of nature's working over fifty thousand years. The blanket bogs of Dartmoor have been formed by the slow rotting of vegetation, and more particularly by the silting action of the many water-courses which, through the ages, have changed from one channel to another, and whose water is by no means confined to a bed, but percolates through the peat cracks. For reasons which are not fully known, active peat formation seems to have stopped over most of the moor, and the soft covering over the rock is shrinking, as dried mud shrinks and shows cracks. On the moor these fissures are now many feet wide between isolated peat hags.

The task of bringing this working proposition to fruition was a challenge which I found very stimulating, and Tessa upheld me. Within a few weeks I had come to a business arrangement with Sol, and the rest of the winter was spent in planning for a start of work in late spring.

There were two distinct commodities to be won from our peat set. There was the fibrous upper layer of material which was sought after by horticulturists and nurseymen, and there was the deep black peat which, when cut and laid out, would dry into fuel blocks as hard as coal. Up to the last stages of production the problems were much the same with both types of peat: they both had to be cut, dried, and transported.

So easy was the cutting that this could be done by hand, but it was not expedient to lay out the blocks on the set. They would get in the way of the cutting, and local sages told me that a wet mist lay so often at that altitude that there was small prospect of drying. A couple of miles down the track, and at an altitude of no more than eight hundred feet, was a broad, swelling promontory of turf, open to the breezes from three sides, firm underfoot, and well drained. Here was the obvious place to lay out the cut peat, and in a hollow near by was the situation for a building in which to store our dried material, and to process it during the wild winter days. We could, I thought, carry the peat from set to drying-ground in tipping lorries.

At this theoretical stage the human equation demanded solution, for on that answer, as always, success or failure was dependent. Sol recommended me to one Bill Waters, who had worked at the set during its brief wartime revival, and who was said to be the most knowledgeable man in all Lydford parish, which was the largest parish in Devon. Bill lived with his mother quite near the start of the peat track. Two brothers also shared the house, and a third ran a one-man garage close by.

Bill Waters was an immensely burly man, quite young in years, but mature in self-possession. His big red face showed frankness and stubbornness. It could also take on a cunning look, though never that slyness which is a frequent Devonian expression. He had at some time experienced training on the *Cutty Sark*, had circumnavigated the globe, and had acquired the resourcefulness of a whole company of castaway Crusoes.

Bill, like me, was bedevilled by the impossibility of the job.

"There's several has had a go at 'un," he said, "and all given up. I'm game for to have a smack if so you be."

We started off with nothing so spectacular as a smack. Bill began to bespeak a working team from the combs and hollows of that thinly peopled countryside, and began to hear of tools and lorries. I came to know well Bill's 'hearing of.' He could hear, so I believe, of any terrestrial commodity within half a day of its first tentative mention. Then there would be a lull of a week or so while he examined it surreptitiously, spoke to people who had had experience with it, played darts and drank with the owner, or with some one who could influence the owner, and finally hypnotized the vendor into accepting a figure below his very minimum. Sometimes the owner was not even a vendor, but in the end he sold just the same.

By March we had acquired a couple of lorries, a Nissen hut, and a lot of hand tools. In London Sol had had a machine constructed to granulate our horticultural peat, and this was now lying under tarpaulins on the open moor. We also had the nucleus of our team at work on the repair of the track and the draining of the cutting into which the lorries would run for their peat loads. What we now required was a building.

Within a few days Bill had heard of a blister hangar on a deserted airfield at the other side of Devon. It was an enormous erection of lattice girders and corrugated-iron sheeting, eighty feet by forty, and twenty-two feet to the top of its arch. We bought it as it stood, and since we had not taken on all our labour, employed a contractor to dismantle it and re-erect, while we lent a hand at the work and did the transportation.

From the very start I was not quite happy about our prospects. True, the moor looked busy enough. There were a dozen men cutting at the peat face at the end of the track up and down which our lorries were shuttling. There were two or three men spreading out the heaps which the lorries had tipped on the turf of the drying-ground. And George and one or other of his two at-home brothers —both of whom had joined us—were busy in the vast interior of the hanger. But the dead weight of the moor bore down on us all. We would see the five-ton loads come swaying and bumping over the skylines which were cut by the track, and the end of a day would tally an impressive tonnage. Yet three-quarters of each load was water, and when our peat was dried to marketable condition its weight was shrunk to a fourth.

The track was a breaker of trucks and an eater of tyres, and despite the cut-rate services of Bill's brother with the garage, the financial toll was heavy. Then the weather was an enemy of the enterprise. This corner of the moor was the first high ground to be struck by that prevailing, moisture-laden south-west wind about which all schoolboys learn. Often enough the heavy clouds slid over our drying ground, but rarely did they fail to unleash their loads above the peat set, their rain lashed to fury by the wind which had come unchecked from the sea.

The men who worked up there were a stout lot, countrymen all, who stayed at their job in all but the wildest weather. They typified the courage and determination which men so often lose when they enter the artificiality of industrial conditions.

However, in spite of natural difficulties we held our own for twelve months. We had persuaded a very big firm of wholesale coal merchants to take our selling agency for both fuel and horticultural peat. The firm advertised our products, booked the orders, collected the money, and paid to us the net figure on which we had agreed. We all understood that we were no more than holding our own, and that nothing less than increased efficiency of production, or a lessening of overhead costs, would allow us to have money in hand.

It was obvious that overheads were unlikely to be reduced, and that, on the contrary, petrol and other taxes were likely to rise, and worst of all that railway freight rates would continue to become more costly, so that the only solution lay in increased efficiency. In many cases efficiency is only bought with money through the medium of mechanical aids, and this was just such a case, where human sinews could not outmatch natural conditions. Mechanization is expensive, and with Sol's help I sought the capital we needed. Then it was that I learned how close a corporation is the investing world, and how cynical. At that time, within a year or two of the War's end, it seemed that the struggle had drained the last drop of our adventurousness, that even those who had not properly known war were content to relax their spirit.

The restrictive practices of the banking houses and the constraint of punitive taxation were to blame in those days for a general lack of enterprise which cramped the country's resurgence. Some of the big financial houses were indeed prepared to loan money to expand and equip going ventures, but these houses to which I applied required to be shown our accounts restrospectively for several years. I could not blame them for this, but did feel that the request was paradoxical, since even the banks would have put up money for us had we had the security of a good long-term trading record to offer. All we could show was a feasible plan which we had put into action, and which, though faltering, was demonstrably doing so through lack of equipment.

However, when I look back upon those days I see that our proposition must have been other-worldly to business-men in city board-rooms. Perhaps I made a mistake in not taking Bill Waters along with me. Had I done so, I dare say some one or other would have helped us if only to retain Bill as local colour.

We worked on as best we could, and made at least one advance from our own resources. It happened that the floor of our cutting began to break up under the manœuvring of our trucks, and to need frequent ballasting. Also, the immediate peat bank which was accessible from the cutting began to lose depth as we ate into it, and became studded with boulders, like raisins in a Dundee cake. Bill Waters and I sank a trial pit in another swelling bank a couple of hundred yards farther into the set, and satisfied ourselves that here we would have several years cutting before we need shift our operations. But there was no way of reaching the new scene with the lorries. The surface of the moor would not support wheels, but shook like a spring mattress at a hard stamp of a foot; nor was it practicable to cut a track down to the bedrock. The one possible means of access was by tramway.

Bill heard of some redundant two-foot gauge tramway, with steel sleepers, at a works near Bristol, and we went over together to bargain for them. It was a good thing that our enterprise was necessarily run on a basis of strict economy, or I certainly would have given rein to my lifelong desire to own a railway. There were miles of line heaped up in the yard. The track was in ready-built sections, just like the ready-to-join-up track of the toy-shops. There were left-hand and right-hand switches, also ready-made like toys. There were splendid little hopper trucks with drop-down lever brakes, and the man who guided us told me that they could even let me have a diesel locomotive.

Now I come to think of it, I might have done well to have bought the lot, and to have laid out a sight-seeing line for tourists. But in the end we compromised sadly for three hundred yards of line, a couple of switches, and four hopper trucks of one cubic yard capacity each. Our motive power was to be the well-known force of human muscle.

We laid our line from the foot of the new bank to the edge of the original cutting, where the rails ended at the lip of the vertical wall of peat. We built out a sort of jetty into the cutting, constructed of old railways sleepers which Bill had heard of, and which was long enough to take one more length of rail. Our plan was that the lorries should drive close up to the side of the jetty, and that our hopper trucks should tip directly into them from their elevation of ten feet or so.

The system worked splendidly in dry weather. The hoppers ran down from the new bank, slowed under their brakes near the jetty, and came to a stop directly above a waiting lorry. The return grade was so gentle that five men could push back an empty truck with little effort, and could switch it into one arm or other of the Y-shaped line layout at the new bank.

The fun began on the first damp day. Bill was up at the set that morning, and, as was his wont, shoved the first loaded truck away from the peat face, clicked over the switch, and leapt on behind for the run across the heather to the jetty. The trip was always exhilarating, and Bill sang like a joyous skylark until the time came to drop the brake lever. The wheels ceased to turn, as was his intention, but the speed of the truck was unabated. It slid as smoothly over the wet rails as a bobsleigh down the Cresta Run. Bill gave a great shout as he threw himself off. The lorry driver, who was smoking peacefully in the cutting below, looked up in time to see the hopper leap over his head like a startled buck, and when its shadow was gone threw himself on his face in the liquid mud, owing to an unfortunately slow nervous reaction.

This incident lent an air of adventure to the trip down the line, and some of us, braving disaster, identified ourselves with those pioneering Americans who built the Iron Road through prairie fires, across collapsing trestle bridges, and under the arrow-clouds of the redskins.

By the second summer our affairs had nearly enough become stabilized. Our team was working as willingly as ever. The lorries ran to and fro up the track, tipping their loads on the drying-ground beside the hangar: the black fuel peat in one place, the spongy horti-cultural in another. The fuel peat was left out, but as the horti-cultural dried it was loaded up, transported into the hangar, and added to the large heap which filled one half of the building as high as the arched top. It was a hard-won harvest, and we were all proud of it.

The granulator was steadily at work close against the sorted pile of peat. The lumps were fed into a conveyor which climbed to a drum in which blunt knives revolved, breaking up the matted material so that it poured through perforations in the drum, was collected in a chute, and fed into sacks. As the filled sacks were weighed, wired at the neck, and labelled to their customers, a mobile conveyor whisked them up on to the lorry which was to deliver them to their home destination, or else to the railway station. The busy scene was deceptively encouraging, for our equip-ment was a swallower of time and labour. These two commodities add up to money.

From peat set to drying-ground, our practice was reasonably efficient. Short of a bucket railway, it could not have been greatly improved. But the trouble began beside the hangar, where each delivered load of sodden peat had to be spread by hand for drying, must later be picked up into a lorry and carted within. There were more efficient methods which could have been used at this stage, but we could afford none of them. The granulator, that child of

Sol's imagination which had been brought to birth with a pencil-sketch on the back of an envelope, was a mechanical marvel in that it worked in spite of so unprofessional a parentage. But it worked only as a marvel. There were on the market granulators of proven heredity, could we but have spared the money to buy one.

Our troubles were not done when at last the granulated horticultural peat was in the sacks, for sacks at that time cost us eighteenpence each, which added thirty shillings to the price of a ton of our product. We added this amount to our invoices, but made it returnable, just as a publican charges for and refunds money on a bottle. However, a bottle does not deteriorate, and sacks which contain peat do. The acid of their contents speedily eats their fibres, and we found that few sacks could make more than two journeys.

The answer to this problem was to press and bale the granulated peat in blocks of one hundredweight. But if we could not afford a new granulator, neither could we a baler.

Meanwhile, we had plenty of customers, for our horticultural peat was of fine quality, and our price on rail low enough to be attractive. The firm of West Country coal merchants who did our marketing operated in a very big way indeed, and by reason of their wide activities were able to place all the orders that we could fulfil. Yet our full production brought no savour of success, for it cost us too dear. It cost us too dear in worry and in heart-breaking labour. It cost us too dear in desire for the tools we could never quite see our way to buying. Yet we had to continue to work in our primitive way, as a desperate swimmer must struggle to keep afloat, knowing that a boat would be his salvation.

It was towards our second winter that I found myself permanently at work on the peat set, and it was now, during a period when Tessa had come from our London home to join me, that we saw the advertisement for the sale of Shallows.

When finally we moved into our new house on the other side of the moor we felt a friendliness and solace which was not in the atmosphere of the peat set. For a while we thought that the moor, so vibrant with the spirits of those who had long since gone, was about to help us; was about to abate the mist and storms which plagued the height where we cut; was about to let our hard-won lorry track remain our gain; was about to let us do our work and earn our bread.

But one winter morning, when I had driven as usual round the end of the moor and had climbed to the hangar, I realized, like a man who has been struck a blow in the face, that the moor made no friends. At some time during the night the wind had swept up to the big building, had driven under it, prised it from its foundations, lifted it in the air, and let it fall.

The hangar lay buckled and twisted; it was, I thought, beyond salvage; yet the moor must have brought out the best in all of us, just as sometimes it had brought out the worst, and all our team swore as men swear against an enemy. Throughout the bitter weeks of lacerating wind, of snow, and of ice-formation, painfully we dismembered the distorted erection. We took it apart until it was resolved into its simple components and lay in its sorted heaps on the frozen ground.

We straightened up the girders with heat and sledge-hammers; we battered into shape the iron sheeting, and Bill heard of replacements for those sheets which had been torn like paper. Through that cruelly bleak spring we built our arches on the earth; hoisted them upright with the pull of lorries dragging a rope over a sheer-legs; braced them with cross-members, we sitting aloft with our hands too cold to feel the bolts which bound the structure and our bodies so cold that we did not mind if we fell or stayed. We spiked the feet of our lattice girders deep in the ground, and set the horizontal bearers in concrete; then over the top of the great structure we slung wire hawsers, and attached their ends to long pickets which were driven in up to their heads.

The hangar weathered the gales which came, and it stands yet. But we had lost many weeks of productive work, and the wrecking was a disaster which accelerated the slow run-down of our resources. Bill Waters toiled harder than ever before, and his loyalty to a failing cause inspired loyalty in his men. Yet, work as we would, we were upon a labour of Sisyphus, for the more peat we bagged and sold the more tyres were ripped; the more lorry-springs were broken; the more granulator repairs were needed; the more sacks were rotted. We were betting on a losing sequence.

N

At this time railway freight rates were frequently increased, and we found that our horticultural customers, who were in the main professional market gardeners, followed their usual course in times of hardship. Your market gardener is not a well-breeched man, dependant as he is on the imponderables of glut, the inequities of distribution, and the greeds of wholesaler and retailer. He reckons to pay last season's bills with this season's income. In times when prices go against him he becomes a master of inactivity.

So he became now. Freight rates reached a height which made peat prices unattractive, and, like threatened hedgehogs, our gardening customers rolled up into protective balls. They needed our peat for mulching into dry ground; for giving to soft fruits and tomatoes, and to hydrangeas and azaleas, the acid soil conditions on which they thrived. Yet peat prices had crept up to a point where the gardeners had to take up their traditional refuge in the good heart of the soil they worked. They decided to live awhile on the accumulated fertility of their plots. In time the price of our produce might fall, or that of theirs might rise; then they would refresh the good earth which had sustained them meanwhile.

We sold our peat set in the third year. It was bought by our selling agents, the wholesale coal merchants, whose resources were equal to the capital needs of the set, and whose transport facilities by rail and ship were able to offer better delivered prices.

I was not happy at the loss of three years' work, and the frustration of a long losing fight. I would have been bitterly resentful of the environment which had been my chief adversary had I not found Shallows.

Shallows was, I suppose, my credit entry against the many debits which the moor had listed against me.

CHAPTER FIFTEEN

*Cord-moss—Ferns—Maize—The onion flower—Meadow sage
—Peas and brooms—Monkey musk and sunflower—Arum lilies
—Life at Shallows*

SOMETIMES the demands of our garden eased for long enough to let us sit and enjoy its beauty and peace. We can only take this relaxation when we have for the moment stemmed the over-vigorous growth of grasses, trees, shrubs, and flowers. This growth, this almost coarse vitality, gives the lie to peace within the garden, and offers a new thought upon the beauty. For all the gentle and glorious blossoms and the many inconspicuous ones, all the root ramblings, all the strangling climbers, all the delicate and ingenious plant mechanisms, are devised to make sure of survival and repro-duction.

Among the growths of a garden thrive vegetable versions of most human vices, with only the one human virtue of tenacity.

Despite sprinklings with a solution of sodium chlorate, our drives and paths still grow their little streaks of cord-moss against the verges where dampness tends to lie. The moss grows from spores which settle on the damp patches. The spores soak up the water and become alive within half a day, throwing out tubes to anchor them-selves among our gravel. Quickly they thrust up a fine thread, from which spring feathery branches, until in mass the frantically alive colony looks solid green. Moss leaves develop among the threads, and presently each cluster of them shows at its centre a dark red knob. This is the male organ of reproduction. The female vessel grows lower down, and a little later on, in order to dis-courage incestuous fertilization. It is shaped like a slender flask which holds within it a solitary egg cell. The cord-moss needs moisture when it is ready for its love-making. The rain-drenched male organ showers spermatozoa into the drops which are trickling down to the female receptacles below. These egg flasks in turn discharge a sugary secretion which attracts the sperms in the drops, and to which they swim and struggle with all the effort of their swimming hairs until they enter the necks of the female vessels and fertilize the eggs.

The moss embryo grows within its flask, clinging to the stem of its mother. It grows until it stretches and snaps off the flask close to its base, and can thereafter use it as a cap for protection during its youth. In time the stalk develops a spore capsule, which is so contrived that it will only open in order to distribute ripened spores when the weather is humid, and even then its mechanism is such that it releases but a few spores at a time, so that each wind gust may carry them to various destinations.

When Tessa and I see the tiny moss patches begin to grow again after the latest path-sprinkling we see them seething with passions and activities which belie their humility and lowly place.

There are many sorts of ferns at Shallows, and these act like the cord-moss. Their spores are held beneath the fronds in round cases which burst violently at the proper time, scattering their contents like small-shot. These spores also thrive upon moisture, and each swells with water until it bursts. Cells build up, at first lengthways, and then sideways to thicken the slender thread, until the structure becomes fan-shaped. All this activity has been to a sexual end, for new male organs, round bodies filled with spermatozoa, appear along the fan's outside edges, and in the centre of the fan grow the female reproductive organs, each one a flask which holds its precious egg.

The fern sperm is another of the swimmers, and withholds its liberation until it can enter water. Now the neck of the female flask opens, and an acid mucilage oozes forth which is an attraction to the indomitable sperms. They struggle towards the liquid, are tempted within the female vessel, and presently fulfil their purpose with the vital egg.

Just as the moss embryo battens upon its mother, so the embryo fern strikes down into the fanlike prothallus which produced its parents. And as the young plant waxes the prothallus languishes and dies, in the same way that age has for so long been trampled by youth in the world of animal life.

At Shallows, where all growing things are so potent, this vigorous preoccupation of plant life with reproduction sometimes frightens us on the rare occasions when we have leisure to sit and listen to the silence. We imagine that the greenery in its many forms is waxing as inexorably as a swift tide; that we are seated within a live organism, like persons swallowed by a leviathan.

Near one of our favourite resting-places is a dug plot which is so sheltered and sunny that we grow maize in it year by year. We often admire the strong plant in its early days. The maize stem grows sturdily, and from its top there presently appears a dangling tassel, as long and fine as an unbound pigtail. At the end of each thread is a pollen-filled male organ, which disseminates its vital dust with the help of the breezes. The pollen dust of the maize is as pertinacious to fulfil its function as are the animal-like, free-moving sperms of moss and fern. The dust drifts downward to neighbouring plants on whose lower parts grow the female flowers, tight wrapped in many-layered green sheaths.

A short tuft of fibres, just like hairs, grows out of the top of each sheath, and exudes a stickiness which traps the drifting pollen. The minute grains, each on its female hair, develop slender tubes which drive for many inches to the very roots of the hairs until they touch the eggs at their base. When union is made the pollen grain passes its nucleus down the tube to achieve consummation.

Tessa and I watch the graceful play of the maize tassels as the breeze idly sways them, but there is no idleness in the plants themselves as each drift of shaken pollen stimulates furious activity in the female sheaths.

Even the soporific summer drone of insects sings of courtship, not sleep. The insects are the cupids of a garden, and those plants which do not use the wind as their courier attract the attention of the cupids with bright colours, scents, and the offer of nectar. Many of them practise remarkable single-minded persistence, and show superlative ingenuity to ensure male and female union. For instance, there is the onion flower, of which Tessa always allows a few to blossom, since she believes that plants grow more healthily from seed which is acclimatized to Shallows. The onion makes the bee's work easy by grouping its flowers in a tight cluster. The flowers open, and six stamens rise, each bearing on its tip the swollen male anther, bursting with pollen. When the pollen has been carried off on the hairy bellies of bees to fertilize elsewhere, the plant's own female organ, the style, protrudes above the level of the exhausted anthers, which offer no danger now of self-fertilization. The stigma at the style's tip exudes its sticky secretion, and the next visiting bee leaves on it the pollen of some near-by plant.

The meadow sage has a more elaborate sex-mechanism than our onion flowers. The questing bee cannot enter the sage flower without pressing a trigger which thrusts two male anthers, laden with pollen, against either side of its back. After a while the male impulse dies, and the female stigma grows until it takes the position which the anthers had held. The meadow sage's stigma has two lobes, and these, tripped by the same trigger, receive the pollen which the bees bring from other meadow sages.

Our peas and brooms are as violent in their reproductive action as the explosive spore-containers of the ferns. Within their flowers both stamens and styles, whose stigmas are ready to receive, are so packed that they are straining to thrust upward, and are only held back by the grip of the flower petals. But an alighting bee upsets the equilibrium. Anthers and stigmas fly up against the insect's furry underside. The anthers shower the bee with pollen, and the stigma receives that which the bee has brought with it from another flower. It receives some of its own flower's pollen too, but it is only the stranger's dust which gains favour with the ovule.

Sterility is as much feared in the plant world as it is in the human life of the East. As a last and desperate measure to achieve reproduction when normal intercourse has failed the monkey musk performs self-pollination. The anthers of the musk are at the base of the trumpet-like flowers, and the stigma projects farther towards the opening. When cupid fails to satisfy the desires of the flower the trumpet is shed. It slides down the column of the style, dusting itself with pollen as it passes the anthers, and lodges itself by the swelling of the open stigma, giving to it the pollen of its own flowers.

If the female styles of the sunflower remain too long with their reproductive urge unsatisfied they curl downward and actively pick up pollen which has come from the anthers of the same floret.

There is no feminine modesty in a garden. The impatient cry is " Cherchez l'homme."

The garden of Shallows, so varied, so warm, so fertile, so well-watered, is vibrant with the loves of growing things.

Near our lily-pool we have a group of arum lilies which look as austerely virginal as nuns. But no one can say what desires seethe behind a cold façade, and the arum lilies are certainly deceivers. Within the sheath of a lily's single petal is a small chamber at the very base. On the floor of the chamber are the female flowers, and above them the male. The entrance to the chamber is guarded by downward-pointing hairs, like the spikes which deter boys from ascending poles.

The female flowers are the first to mature. At once the temperature of the chamber rises, and the plant gives off an odour which attracts midges to the comfort of the warmth within. When the insects have been procured they find that the hairs in the opening of the flower chamber keep them prisoner. They clamber dazedly around, fertilizing the females with the pollen which they have brought with them, and collecting from the males more pollen to carry away. When desire is appeased the females feed nectar to the midges to strengthen them before release; the barrier of hairs shrivels, and the insects crawl out into the open air to bear the fresh pollen to another arum lily.

All the machinations to a reproductive end are not, of course, peculiar to the garden of Shallows. It is simply our misfortune that the norm of fertility and survival for which nature caters is not our norm. Nature has arranged to give parachutes to wind-blown seeds; and for insects to visit flowers; she has also arranged that the seeds of dodder and burdock shall cling to our clothes so that we may pick them off and drop them on fresh ground; she has arranged that the seeds of blackberries, strawberries, raspberries, and currants are not affected by their passage through the crops of birds. All these fall on fertile soil at Shallows, and reproduce their kind with the old-fashioned liberality which is described in the pages of the Old Testament.

We can explain the animal facts of life without embarrassment, but hesitate over the lusts of flowers.

It is mayhem which saves the house of Shallows from absorption by the garden. The natural plant increase is so great that it defeats itself, just as the populations of some teeming countries in the end consume their surplus through famine and plague. If it is not concupiscence in a garden, it is the slow murder of strangling climbers, of ravenous spores, and of plants and shrubs and trees which use every shift and device to achieve survival, just as desperate and unmoral people will struggle with each other among the debris of a shipwreck.

And yet we feel that our garden is a clean and peaceful place despite the cold analysis which we sometimes make of the goings-on. At Shallows we are tempted to philosophize, placed all alone as we are between the stars, so busily and purposefully gyrating, and the plant-life which follows a cycle equally precise. When we look up into the coldness of the night sky we can understand that nothing may escape from the immensity of it, and that the dust of shattered stars is the raw material of new worlds. Just so in our garden death breeds life, and nothing is lost.